the inward journey

the

inward

journey

BY DORIS PEEL

1953

HOUGHTON MIFFLIN COMPANY BOSTON
The Riverside Press Cambridge

Grateful acknowledgment is made to The
Christian Science Monitor for permission to use
an episode first published by them.

The author also acknowledges with thanks
permission granted by the publishers to quote
from the following works:

Complete Poems of Robert Frost published by
Henry Holt and Company, Inc.

Poems by Emily Dickinson edited by Martha
Dickinson and Alfred Leete Hampson, published
by Little, Brown & Company.

"The Second Coming" in Collected Poems by
William Butler Yeats, used by permission of
Mrs. W. B. Yeats and the Macmillan Company
of Canada; the Macmillan Company of New
York; and Macmillan & Company, Ltd., of
England.

Perseus in the Wind by Freya Stark published
by John Murray, Ltd.

"Message to Siberia" by Aleksandr Pushkin,
translated by Max Eastman, as it appears in
The Poems, Prose and Plays of Pushkin published by Random House, Inc.

The Riverside Press · CAMBRIDGE, MASSACHUSETTS · PRINTED IN THE U.S.A.

To those friends
in several countries
who constitute
with their courage and faith
the advance citizenry of a new world

Do not lose heart; we are all here
HERMANN BROCH

Only the inward journey is real.

ELLA MAILLART

All you continentals of Asia, Africa, Europe, Australia,
    indifferent of place!
All you on the numberless islands of the archipelagoes
    of the sea!
And you of centuries hence when you listen to me!
And you each and everywhere whom I specify not, but
    include just the same!
Health to you! good will to you all, from me and
    America sent!
Each of us inevitable,
Each of us limitless — each of us with his or her right
    upon the earth,
Each of us allow'd the eternal purports of the earth,
Each of us here as divinely as any is here.

WALT WHITMAN

We carry with us the wonders we seek without us.

SIR THOMAS BROWNE

I further and further went anon,
    As each I still surveyed,
And further yet — yea, on and on,
And all the men I looked upon
    Had heart-strings fellow-made.

I traced the whole terrestrial round,
    Homing the other side;
Then said I, "What is there to bound
My denizenship? It seems I have found
    Its scope to be world-wide."

THOMAS HARDY

contents

mid-journey

So they had them to the top of
an high hill, called Clear . . . .
Then they assayed to look, but
. . . they could not look steadily through the glass; yet they
thought they saw something like
the gate, and also some of the
glory of the place.

PILGRIM'S PROGRESS

mıð-jouRney

EVERY NOW AND THEN, when one is traveling, with time and
space so intermixed that the earth flows past as fluently as the
hours and the hours are shaped into a thousand scenes —
every now and then there can be a passage that for all its
movement is somehow a pause. Perhaps it is determined by an
inner necessity: the brilliant flood has become too much. Or
perhaps it is a logical summing-up point. Moment upon moment and mile upon mile happen; accumulate; in some fashion
coalesce; until, sprung from a necessity of its own, there the
sum is — the seizable significance. Perhaps that's the way
of it, although I'm none too sure; for the feeling isn't really
of something amassed, but of something penetrated: as if
through the streaming stuff of a journey, a central stillness and
substance had been touched.

At any rate, they occur, these now-and-then times. And
even as they do, one can be aware of them. So much in life
must be grasped in retrospect — the proportions discerned
and the values fixed only as the light derived from an experience is cast back on it from a stage ahead. But sometimes a

3

happening is possessed as it happens; is reaped as it flowers. Even as it begins there's the inward sign. "*Be still! Receive —* " one can say to oneself.

As in Austria it was, on the Gross Glockner.

Several months were behind us, and a number of countries: a journey multitudinously crowded with people — and with the issues, the tensions, the related urgencies everywhere to be acknowledged and incessantly discussed: the mental map of Europe as well as the physical one. The previous morning Germany had been left. Berlin, braced under the latest of its crises, with Regina and Klaus and all the other friends, and the Russian in Gerhardt Eisler's headquarters, and Ernst, of the Volkspolizei, who had come to my rescue. Friedl had been left, in her Hessian village; and Hildegard and the rest of the Munich group; and Hans's family at the inn in Berchtesgaden. Ahead of us, flowing without set design, were several more months and some thousands of miles. Yugoslavia, unknown, was about to be explored — Yugoslavia that was to mean, in the ensuing weeks, Drago, Viktor, Miloje, Koca; Dimitri who had fought from the outset with Tito, and Katya who had punted on the Isis at Oxford; officialdom in Belgrade; and Zagreb parties; Macedonian dancers, with their drums and scimitars, and high in the stony mountains of Dalmatia, peasants — bearing themselves like ragged grandees, with arms upflung in an immemorial salute — shouting out "Zdravo!" in instant welcome. These were before us; yet to be known.

At the moment, having stopped for lunch in Salzburg, we were headed pell-mell, or so we assumed, for Trieste, where Kip was to join us from Venice. (With his tinkerlike equipment of razor blades, toothbrushes, soap and film; an invaluable smattering of Serbo-Croat; and a capacity, almost mystical, to wrest hard-boiled eggs from the most remote, barbaric and undenizened wilds.) The immediate run we hadn't given much thought to; I suppose because so much else had been happening. There was Trieste, plain enough — downward, and to the right, on the Adriatic; and although there was some bumpy-looking stuff on the map, the actual distance could be managed, we judged, in the allotted time if none of it were lost.

So there we were, with Salzburg behind us. And it was one of those incandescent afternoons.

As we drove, with the top down, in the little English car, the air was a long warm flow in one's face, bearing with it all the ripeness of the sunlit earth, meadow and orchard and high dark firs. The river was a lovely gilded coil, between slopes brightly burnished and steeply pitched where the belled cattle stood — far up and still — like painted toys, among small gay flowers. A summertime world, deep-toned, relaxed. Until, as we journeyed, there was a gradual change. The mountains were growing higher; and more severe. And late, quite late, in the afternoon we found ourselves suddenly flagged to a stop, at the side of the road and in front of a lodge, and asked — for some reason imperfectly grasped — if everything was in order: were we all set?

"Certainly," we said. And wondered why the Authority, with a reassuring hand, should pat the bonnet of the Morris Minor. (When, in due course, the deed was done, a little sticker was pasted like a decoration on the windshield; and always after that, through those following months, whenever we saw on another car the sign of the Gross Glockner, we felt like fellows of the same princely order.)

The hand was waved. We were on our way. And now the road under us was really taking flight. Up it went, up, in a great gleaming reach; so superbly looped that everything in sight could be seen twice, from opposite directions. There was no further evidence of man or beast. Only occasionally was there another car; and after a time not even that. The sun was cut off; the light drained away. And gradually there was the familiar realization. Something special had been entered upon, something had begun. *"Be still! Receive —"* said the inward voice.

We were all alone. Magnificently alone. In a vast, stark, de-personalized world: growing colder and colder with a purity of cold that was like the air from some stainless and icy star. Something gleamed ahead of us, unearthly pale: torrential and yet fixed — "A glacier," Stephen said. If we spoke it was quiet-voiced; and after a while, as we climbed and climbed into height above height, with the dusk turned to darkness and the sky gone black, we didn't speak at all, having no further need to. For here was the ancient, the immemorial awe. Here silence upon silence, until, in the night, the stupendous upthrust of the massive peaks became the ultimate resolution of sound, music beyond music, word beyond word.

We were driving to Trieste, but Trieste ceased to be. All the days, summer-brilliant, dissolved; were gone. People were gone; and the issues, the policies — the endless machinations and the desperate needs and the fear coiled serpentlike in millions of hearts. Flags were gone; and frontiers; and two-worlds. For here was the stuff of a planet, a universe: an elemental order beyond name, out of time: sovereign and indisseverably existing as itself. We climbed and climbed in the bitter cold, in the purity of an air unscarred by man. And everything except this was a myth surmounted, with seductions as extinct as threat or curse. One was simplified as stone, and star-immune. One was loosed utterly from all that had been left: from the need to grapple, to strive, to act, to mingle with the groping or even, any more, to suffer the awareness of humanity and its search.

The mountains were the world, and the world all space. And then, suddenly, the space was fixed. Suddenly, above us and immediately ahead, there was a spark; then a glow; then the shape of a lodge.

And at once, at the sight of it, we were rigid with cold. We were jarred into the consciousness of hours and miles and the glacial emptiness and ourselves all alone; and stopping the car, we stumbled out, making our way clumsily across the frozen ground to a door that opened for us almost as we knocked. And there, like a miracle, hardly to be grasped, was light — warmth — the magnificent smell of food; there, sounding strange and beautiful to the ear (as if for an uncounted time unheard) were voices again; the voices of a small company of travelers like ourselves, halted by the night and pitched against sky.

Our inescapable — and indispensable — fellow man.

In the morning there was a fog as dense as wool. We might have been ghostily adrift on a ship. And sitting there together in the warm safe room we exchanged information across steaming breakfasts with an easy but unencroaching acceptance of one another. Here we all were, a compact little world of us — haphazardly assembled at the top of the world. The South African, the French couple, the family from London; the several Germans and the Greek boy teamed with the Norwegian and the pair of laconic, motorcycling G.I.'s.

We spoke what we could in the languages shared; we penciled, for comparison, on outspread maps the routes we had come by and the journeys ahead. The camaraderie of the marooned intermeshed us all. But nothing beyond this was either evident or sought. No special rapprochement was ours by right. For although we were on mountains no one of us had arrived by grace of his own muscle and wind and nerve; no passion had been involved; no risk or cost. We weren't of that unique and heroic breed, the Mallorys and Whympers and Guido Reys, nor of any company bound by a skill or craft, or an incommunicable dream, or a high ordeal. No challenge had been ours; nothing trackless had been traversed. Whatever daring there was or mastery of stroke it resided in the achievement of the road itself (to be chalked up, alas, to the men of the Third Reich) and in the conceiving of that which had borne us here, metal and fuel obedient to the will. What had once been triumph for the hero-man now was held casually by anyone at all. The child with his toy; the Frenchwoman knitting.

And it was this, one realized, that essentially bound us. Diversified though we were, we shared the same hour: both privileged and penalized by the nature of it.

For although so much — so miraculously wrought — was easily ours, we had forfeited with the endowment the old sense of miracle. With the challenge gone something of the wonder had gone too. (What heights were there left for a little boy who before he could walk straight had been given the Alps?) There was no island any more to set foot on first; no realm to be scanned in a wild surmise. We had used up the earth, and the seven seas, and even the airy streets of the sky. We were driven back now (if the challenge, the adventure, were what we sought) upon a different order of exploration and risk. For the jungles and the crags and the burning sands must, now, be tackled elsewhere. Across the territories of the

mind we must find our way; through the strange and hazardous places of the heart.

Here we all sat, safe and warm.

And yet — were the safety and the warmth really all?
Wasn't there, in spite of them, the other thing too?

For as the morning lengthened and we were still fogbound,
gradually there happened what inevitably happens when
people, nameless to one another, are for any stretch of time
isolated in a group. Everyone became somehow intensely real:
not so much "known" as acutely acknowledged. On a street
corner all could have passed unperceived. But here, set off by
circumstances and space, each assumed the proportions of a
figure in a Morality: at once simplified and symbolic; particularized and yet expanded into more than himself. And
touched, too, by an ancient light.

For although, true enough, we hadn't won our way here,
nevertheless — here we were, all far from home. We might
not be heroes, but we were travelers at least. Even marked as
such by certain of the signs: this ease with one another, and
this patience before the incalculable conduct of the elements;
even the acceptance, without ado, of mattresses on the floor the
previous night. We weren't, any of us, where we "belonged."
And whatever the motive or impulse had been that had
brought us forth on our various ways it must, at some point,
be luminously allied to something as old as man's first step.
At some point we were touched to a timeless company.

And all mixed together (from tale and fact) one thought of
Ulysses on his wine-dark sea, and Marco Polo setting sail, and
St. Paul's stormy passage from Crete to Malta; the Pilgrims
of Chaucer, and Dante's dark, labyrinthine search, and the
Children of Israel magnificently afoot; and Drake, Cortez,

Scott, Dick Whittington; Gulliver and Don Quixote and
Pantagruel in Cathay; and Vikings and Crusaders; and Tom
Sawyer's river voyage, and St.-Exupéry traversing, alone and
high, the radiant spaces of his own awareness. All mixed together, the literal and the dreamed: from the first settlers
sighting the rockbound coast to Alice, down her rabbit hole,
pushing open doors.

Somehow we were allied. By motive; by impulse or cloudy
urge. Perhaps as no more than fugitives from the familiar; or
as holidayers only — opening our arms to the splendid multiplicity of the earth's delights. Or perhaps we sought, each in
his own way (for who can tell how it is for another?), that
horizon still lying beyond what is found: that country where
"the sun shineth night and day . . . out of the reach of Giant
Despair" where none who have managed to journey to it can,
any more, "so much as see Doubting Castle. . . . "

The morning lengthened; we were held in the room. And
then, gradually, beyond the windows, there was a thinning, a
pulsating movement of the fog. And suddenly a great lifting
was taking place. With a stupendous soundlessness, without
a sign, it began. And all of us, in a rush, were out of doors. All
of us together, as there — clean around — in rank upon rank,
radiant, Genesis-like: as if but this instant struck from Mind
— sprang mountain beyond mountain and yet more of them
and more, mountains beyond anything one had previously
conceived of until in an outflying foam of cloud, in a glitter of
sun, a whole universe of peaks came consummately plain.

And no longer did it matter how we had arrived. Or that
thousands before us had come the same way. There was only
this; only now; without process or past. With all of it seen as
freshly as if never before seen. For each, after all, is his own
first time. Each, at some inmost point in himself, must stand,

must exist, at a common start. Not lost in a sequence; but singly sprung. The primal pilgrim — whether early or late: with the discoveries undiminished by the discoverers who have passed; the verities still dawnlike; the very leaf and bird as green, as singing, anywhere found, as bird and leaf in the first of springs. . . .

When we turned, looking around us, seeing one another, we smiled quickly in some kind of acknowledgment. For here were the mountains — everywhere in sight: all flung, affirmatively, like a great ringing shout, above the dense and shadowy valleys of Europe. And belonging to no one — or belonging to all. That was what one saw, that was what one felt, standing there in the stupendous blue and white blaze. To him who climbs high enough there are no frontiers. "Mine" and "yours" irradiate into "ours." For we all stood together, heirs of the same light.

Before heading down again to the world below.

JOURNEY ACROSS A LINE

Something there is that doesn't love a wall. . . .
ROBERT FROST

Brotherhood here in the strange world is the rich and
Rarest giving of life and the most valued:
Not to be had for a word or a week's wanting.
ARCHIBALD MACLEISH

Let him (a man) choose for himself with such care
that he may not fear to give his reasons. But be
ready, like some honest countryman, to point out
a direction to those who wish to travel in the region that he knows: and then he will find himself
in a company larger than he had ever thought, of
such as like the roughness and adventure of his
way. And let this be his tolerance, that he knows
those who travel by other paths to be out of hearing. . . . And if he is inclined to missionary under-
takings, let him remember that his knowledge of
the country is useful only to those who wish to
travel in his path.

Tolerance cannot afford to have anything to do
with the fallacy that evil may convert itself to good.
FREYA STARK

We hear the bawlings and din, we are reached at by divisions,
jealousies, recriminations on every side,
They close peremptorily upon us to surround us, my comrade,
Yet we walk unheld, free, the whole earth over, journeying
up and down. . . .
WALT WHITMAN

JOURNEY ACROSS A LINE

THE FIRST TIME I started off for Berlin I never got there at all.

Instead, in a chill and ambiguous dawn, Friedl and I — then traveling together — were domestically making cocoa for a group of armed Volkspolizei at some nameless point, in the Russian Zone, where the previous evening we had been taken off a train.

This, for me, was a revelatory mishap. For although one can read and read about something, and say, "Yes, that must be so," with the sensibilities and the imagination serving one well, always there is the dimension only to be found in the experience itself. Even when it comes to the look of things. For in spite of what films and photographs can tell, how different the impact of the actual scene. As I'd realized, again, some weeks before this — at midnight it had been, at the station in Cologne: with Friedl running suddenly out of space (it was nine years since we'd seen each other) and Kurt following her, waving his wildflowers.

All through the gilded late afternoon, from the Nord Express, the Belgian countryside had been streaming past. The

15

narrow lanes, the canals, the fields of beautiful sculptured cab-
bages, purplish, with a bloom to them like grapes or plums,
and the steep, tangerine-colored roofs of houses that might
have been drawn by a Grandma Moses. Later on, in the dusk,
across meadows growing misty and cobbled streets, postage-
stamp windows had begun to glow out. "My hearth, my
home, my center and circumference" — they had seemed to
say, those little lights. (But how vulnerable all such things
in our world! how in a moment scattered and extinguished!)
Night had come; and at one point the sound of the train had
changed, there was a sudden hollow, irregular clatter; and
forcing one's gaze beyond the reflection of ourselves — five
wraiths riding in a phantom compartment — one had seen
from the window an inky gleam. The Englishman, looking
too, had said, "The Rhine." A Quaker, and a man both sensitive and experienced, he had suffered, one judged, his own
kind of loss: the world's evil had become too much. Earlier
he had said, "This benighted race!" and had added, at a protest, "I don't need to be told that my attitude, for a Christian,
is indefensible. Or to be told, either, that the Germans aren't
the first people in history who've tried to destroy the spirit
of man. But they're the first *artists*. And for this I find myself unable to forgive them." And when somebody else had
spoken of the Russians, he had said, "The Russians act out
of darkness. The Germans were of us, of civilized man."

At Aachen I had been left alone in the compartment; and
at Cologne, after midnight — in a silent, cavernous, faintly
lit shell, with the whole sky starrily exposed overhead — the
few other passengers who had remained on the train had
rapidly dispersed; had dissolved, it seemed, into the secrecy of
the night; for when, following Kurt, we stepped outside there
had been nobody left but our three selves.

We had stood in some sort of open space. And before us, more immediate than I'd expected it to be, had loomed without detail the great cathedral: a stupendous uprush of darkness in the dark: somehow, one had felt, translated into sound — so that for a moment one could have sworn one was hearing it: a magnificent windlike roaring into the sky. Then, turning, I had stared around. And there it had been — the actual scene.

There it was. And what I felt, I think, at that first impact in the dead of night, was a shock of surprise. For it was as if it had all been seen before; not as literal fact; not realistically; but in the subjective terms of contemporary painting. These violent shapes, these huge, outlandish formations upon the air, abstract and yet massive, vehement-looking, with a kind of nightmare beauty to them — for years the eye had been instructed in it all.

"But how beautiful!" I found myself saying out loud.

And then felt appalled, at having uttered such words — trying to grasp that these hulks and cavities, this de-personalized, derelict world under the stars had been lit once by the normalities of living. There had been doors, at which postmen had knocked with letters, and stairs, up and down which children had run; there had been warmth and light and music and flowers, and the sound of dishes, and the smell of food; in those meaningless sockets curtains had hung. . . . But the gap was too great between that and this. It was like trying to convert the bleached bones on the prairie into the full-fleshed buffalo or the racing horse.

"By night, yes," Kurt agreed, "then it can be poetry. But by day you will find it turned to prose." And we walked down something that must, once, have been a street like ordinary streets; walking without sound, one realized suddenly, for it was dirt not pavement underfoot. "This," said Friedl, "was the Piccadilly of Cologne." And on either side of us (achieved, it seemed, in some moment of monstrous but brilliant lunacy) were the stark thrusts of masonry, signifying nothing, and those sudden, those extraordinary downpouring effects — torrential masses of girders and stone held in a kind of suspended crash, as if all had been falling thunderously through space and then, mysteriously, had been stopped, held fast, transfixed like this between two states, structure and debris.

Transfixed and adamant; there the ruins were. And an impression grew that one was unprepared for: a sense of the positiveness, the aggressiveness, of what was left. Tons upon tons of bombs had been dropped; but there was still something here; even something going on, for one saw now — far up in the huge and hollowed shapes — little cores of light; torches of some sort. There was no one to be seen. But there was a sound coming forth. A sound of drilling that must, I suppose, have been going on steadily and that, once heard, altogether dominated the ghostly air. We halted, listening. The drilling drove into one's bones. Then somewhere farther off and unseen in the night there was a dull crumble, a sudden giving way, accelerating gradually into an avalanche-roar. Not an enemy now, but the workmen of Cologne. Bringing down the stubborn stuff of their city.

When the worst had been done, there was all this still to do! For the first time one saw it, plain, like that.

"Underneath," Kurt said, "lie thousands upon thousands of us — " But thousands, millions, were left; were here. When the worst had been done, anywhere on earth, they crawled out again, they stood up, they went on. None of us could get rid of all the rest.

Since then, a curious perversion had set in. Now, after weeks of ruined things, it was the intact, the normal appearance of a place to which the eye had to make a deliberate adjustment. For nobody can go on and on being shocked. And strange arrangements are to be arrived at, one finds, with one's own sensibilities.

In Berlin, Regina and Klaus were waiting for us; they were to meet our train at eight o'clock the next morning.

It was our own decision, to go by train. For in the air one transcends the hindrances of the earth in a way that is at once both true and misleading. The frontiers dissolve; yet remain to be reckoned with. And since the point and purpose of this particular journey was to experience intimately the common order of things, we had, from the first, steered clear of the specialized — of Occupation personnel and professional observers (easily enough done at our level of discomfort): stopping off in villages and sleeping on floors and trudging miles over cobblestones, rubble and pine needles in our grubby raincoats and with two small bags. So it was the ground for us rather than the sky. And because Friedl, as a German, couldn't travel with me on the Allied express with its military escort, it seemed, at the time, natural enough for me to go with her on a German train. "Two to Berlin," we simply said. In the Frankfurt station at the ordinary ticket office. And bolted down the platform to jump aboard.

It was early evening but late in the year. The light soon failed. And since we hadn't lately had much sleep, we proceeded to settle ourselves in for the night: shoes taken off, scarves tied around heads, and our faces (alas) cleaned with cold cream. We neatly spread towels over those little seat

ends which, put together, make a pillow of sorts. We closed
the door of the compartment and turned off the light and
stretched ourselves out, one on each side.

As usual, it was a little while — in spite of the tiredness —
before I could stop feeling Germany in my head. Invisible,
it remained vehemently a pressure upon the mind: Bach-and-
Belsen, endlessly posed. Then the sense of it blurred; one fell
asleep. Only to be awakened, some time later, by the opening
of the door and the corridor's dimmed light breaking in. It
was the customs police; German; and happily avuncular —
for he said at once, in a reassuring way, "Everything looks
much too dainty to disturb!" and scribbled with his piece of
chalk on our bags. We drowsed off again; then again were
wakened. It was somebody else, also in uniform, and this time,
it appeared, collecting all newspapers. "Whatever for?" I
wanted to know. Because, we were told, it was forbidden to
take newspapers into the Russian Zone.

After that we must really have gone to sleep; for several
hours went by. And one dreamed on and off the kind of
dreams that, for once, were no more surrealist than the fact
itself. The piece of a house, freakishly spared, everything on
each side of it struck into chaos, with petunias in a window
box and a polished doorknob; or the gold-and-vermilion flash
of a fresco (the supper table, the disciples, the haloed head)
serene in a wild downfall of Romanesque walls. . . . One slept
and dreamed, going to Berlin. Then the next thing one knew
we were both rearing up, startled, dazed, in a harsh glare of
light.

The train had stopped. It was pitch-black outside. And
immediately at hand in our open doorway, saying, "Passports,
please" — looking tidy, compact, and quintessentially prosaic,
rather as Mr. Molotov used to look, under crystal chandeliers,

at San Francisco — stood a Russian inspector in civilian clothes.

Friedl was the first to produce her papers. They were taken, scrutinized, and handed back to her. Then mine were held out. And almost instantly it was apparent that something was amiss.

The inspector, clinically turning the pages, said several times and in a rapid voice something that sounded like, "Teck, teck, teck — "

"What is teck, teck, teck?" I sociably enquired. And the next moment could have bitten off my tongue! For the sally (fatuous enough to begin with) had as it was uttered a kind of dreadful sprightliness: like a ping-pong ball against an expanse of granite. It pinged, then dropped; with an ignominious thud.

Little feminine pleasantries — that much was plain! — were from now on inexorably out.

The inspector, without a glance, had stepped back into the corridor. He spoke sharply. "Police!" he said.

It wasn't, ordinarily, a word to jump at. London Bobbies had benignly graced one's childhood and the Irishmen of New York, if a tougher breed, had done nothing more drastic than from time to time bawl one out for a tendency to jaywalk. A domesticated word. Rather like "postman." But Friedl's face, in an instant, had gone closed-looking; taut. The nine years stood suddenly between us.

In the corridor two men promptly appeared. Booted and with rifles slung across shoulders, they wore the dark blue uniforms that in due course one was to see a fair amount of, this way and that. The Volkspolizei: the People's Police. (With Ernst himself a long time ahead.)

While we sat there, glossy-nosed, in stocking feet, they con-

ferred briefly, their voices lowered. Then, "Out!" we were
told — in a tone as devoid of hostility as concern: so de-
personalized, and yet incisive, that it seemed almost surgical.
"No permit. You must go back," the inspector amplified.

"Back!" we repeated.

It must be midnight at least! Regina and Klaus were to
meet us in the morning, and besides — and to the point — it
wasn't so! Properly and quite legibly stamped in my passport
was permission to enter West Berlin.

I started, bracing myself, to proclaim the fact; but, "Quick,
please, quick!" we were being enjoined. An air of the most
awful urgency had been generated: all in a twink and by no
recognizable means. It caught one up, like a strong freak
wind, so that there we were — in a blind sort of way thrusting
on shoes and blundering into coats with the whole train, the
whole railway schedule, one assumed, immobilized by us; almost anything at stake. At the last moment, stopping dead, I
put on lipstick. Whether in the cause of vanity or democracy,
it was the one gesture; a poor thing but mine own. Then lug-
ging our bags which seemed suddenly full of pig iron we
stumbled through the corridor and down the steps. Down
into the alien, the enigmatic night.

There appeared to be an unnecessary number of police.
The darkness swarmed with them — all stomping about, with
the glint of guns, and doing one couldn't begin to grasp what.
Their faces were sooty-eyed, indecipherable discs; when they
spoke they shouted and they kept on saying "Quick!" as we
crunched, surrounded by them, the full length of the train.
The ground felt cindery underfoot. The train itself stood
ominously quiet as if everyone in it were sitting tight as a fist
or had turned, prudently, the other way. There was nothing
whatever to be seen anywhere. Until, having passed the final

coach, we were herded across the tracks to some sort of vaguely outlined shape above which glowed (beautiful but unpromising) an illumined red star.

The room we were taken into was small and bare; so thoroughly nondescript that attention was undividedly fixed on those in it. For we weren't, as we'd supposed, the only ones. Nine other people had been ordered off. Nine people who were to assume, in the hours that followed, a curiously dramatized kind of identity — like figures in a masque, nameless to the end, mysteriously assembled to perform their parts.

There we all stood, eyes smarting in the brightness. The young couple warily holding close to them two small children, wobbly with sleep; the thin girl, in a raincoat, hands thrust in pockets; and the elderly woman with her air of meticulous propriety, neat veil, darned gloves, umbrella on arm; the two quiet men, apparently friends, and the third one, younger and excessively handsome, bearing himself godlike (Siegfried to a turn), who was dispensing with such enormous authority and aplomb explanation and advice to everyone else that we assumed he was here as an official intermediary until the fact transpired that he, too, had been caught out.

Seated behind a desk was one of the police. Others passed in and out, still stomping, still shouting — young men, all of them, it now could be seen, although they remained at this stage indistinguishable from one another. Impersonal, peremptory, aggressively unsmiling. As the women were, too; for two girls in uniform had come tramping through the door. They unslung their rifles and tramped out again: looking as one imagined women guards to have looked at Dachau, Belsen, Ravensbrück. And one thought suddenly — so this was how it was! For these were Germans. No Russian was now present.

And because of the speed with which everything had happened, and the outlandishness of the hour, and the glare of light, one found oneself cast into a queer confusion. Were these Nazis? — were they Communists? — what was one faced with?

Everybody at this point was clamoring in a chorus: protesting, demanding to know what was wrong; and the young man behind the desk, with permits and passports in a pile before him, shouted, "Do you all understand why you're being sent back?"

"No!" cried everyone, beginning to shout too.

Explanations were then given, in a chaotic sort of way. And it wasn't until afterwards, until the whole thing was over, that one wondered why on earth there'd been chaos at all. For the facts, if quixotic, were communicable enough. The elderly woman's permit lacked a date, for instance — the fault of the official who had issued it to her; she must return to Heidelberg to have the date put on. ("But I have no money! How can I?" she kept asking. For months, we were to learn, she had saved for this journey, to be with a daughter who was about to have a child.) And the young couple, who had been insisting over and over that a member of their family just the previous week had visited their parents with precisely the same papers that had, at the same time, been issued to them, were told that the requirements had changed since last week. They must return to Stuttgart. And the girl to Düsseldorf. And so on for each of the other passengers. Each was somewhere or other at fault; however picayune the point involved. The Russian on the train, it was necessary to recognize, had acted rigidly within his rights; or rigidly, rather, in accordance with his orders. Given regulations at once inflexible and arbitrary, this was how regulations must work. And there was a sudden relief — in tumbling to this. The procedure, if de-humanized, was a procedure of sorts. There were rules; they were adhered to. The trouble being, it would seem, that the rules were made up as they went along!

At any rate, something felt graspable now. The situation was concrete; not goblinesque fantasy.

Although my own case, to the end, was still hanging in the air. (We were to find that no American had been held here before; probably none had been idiot enough to come this way.) My press card, my vaccination certificate, my Vienna permit, a letter from the State Department and a note from my mother were all studied in succession and with the blind intensity of those who know not what they peruse. "What is it? What's wrong?" I wanted to know — almost anxious to be found at fault, like the rest of the group, in order to keep the circumstances solidly defined; but it became obvious that at this level nobody knew.

Afterwards, the reason was easily enough determined. I was on quite the wrong train; I had no military orders; the case against me could hardly have been more thorough!

Then suddenly all the papers were being returned to us; and we found ourselves hustled by half a dozen of the police, and again with that mysteriously generated urgency, into another room — a long one, dismal and dank, lit to no more than a kind of dusk and with nothing whatever in it but long wooden benches against each wall. An Existentialist play could have settled right in; more than ever, indeed, we seemed dreamed-up "characters," in some sort of inexpertly directed drama. For what one felt at the outset was to be felt until the end: a curious lack of any focal point — no central authority or specific intention; no figure one could either appeal to or defy.

Another train, we were told, the one coming from Berlin, would pause here briefly some hours from now; if it was "possible" we'd be allowed to board it. That was all; such as it was. And a few minutes later we heard our own train.

Slowly, inexorably, with gathering speed, it was pulling out; and everyone sat motionless, with a listening look: hanging on to the last faint sound of it in the night. Then it was gone. The silence was absolute.

In the doorway, with their guns, were stationed two of the police. Nobody spoke; but something now had become evident in the room, an undercurrent of adjustment, a kind of settling in: as if for a voyage, and by practiced hands. The tottering children, wrapped in coats, were curled up closely between their young parents. The girl, farther away, had made a prop of her luggage; she was leaning back, very tired-looking, with stains under her eyes, while the elderly woman, also seated by herself — who had been reading and doggedly re-reading her permit, as if by sticking to it she could somehow conjure the date into evidence — now stopped reading, sat immobile, hands lax. The two quiet men were putting on their overcoats (it was cold already and was to get much colder) and the younger one, still exuding that unwarranted air of superiority to the common lot, had unfastened his suit-case and was taking out a knife, a loaf, a sausage. . . .

There was something curiously facile in it all. Not a word had been exchanged, but everyone with the same fluency and within the same few minutes appeared to have passed from a state of protest to an almost relaxed conceding of defeat. These people, one recognized, had been conditioned to "accept"; and again there was that sense of a different order of experience. For it was a kind of incredulity that one felt one-self: an impulse to stand up and sensibly say, "Oh, but come now, *really!* Let's not be absurd — "

Outside, through the windows, there was total blackness. It

was night, one told oneself — like any other night; if one stepped out into it there'd be ground underfoot and sky there somewhere with the immemorial stars. But one couldn't step out! Here the literal fact! And here one sat, like everybody else!

Another guard, a third one, had come suddenly into the room. He strode over, stood in front of me, and demanded my passport.

I handed it to him, and then asked, "Why?"

The sequence, of course, was flagrantly wrong! So, "Why?" I again asked, rather more loudly.

"It will be given back to you. Later, when you leave."

"Yes, but why do you want it now?"

"So," I was told, "you won't run away."

And at this, everybody — including the police — burst out laughing. However one looked, perched there on the bench, it could hardly have been like the sort of person who would go hoofing off, in an unknown zone, with guns and boots swarming in pursuit.

But it was a spasm, that was all — the ironic laugh. A moment afterwards it was difficult to believe it had occurred.

Away went my passport; there was silence again.

And now all the tales one had recently been told, tale after tale by German after German (not to be discounted but to be evaluated, too, within the context of a rumor-ridden, guilt-complicated people — all too prone, one had soon enough realized, to say, "Look! See how much worse they are than we were!") began luridly to well up in the imagination. The last faint cry, and the impenetrable aftermath! The cells — the salt mines —

At which point there entered, with a considerable clatter, the Russian soldier.

He was a short fellow, rosy, with a young peasant face. And, "Where is the American?" he demanded loudly.

"Here," I said, bracing myself, heart in mouth.

He clattered over and planted himself flat in front of me. He was beaming; he was radiating an incredulity of his own. "Not a real American? Not a *real* one!" he exclaimed.

Friedl said quietly, "He's never seen one before."

Certainly the young Russian appeared fascinated to the core. "An *American!*" he kept on wonderingly repeating. "Here! right here!" Then, "Prove it," he ordered, suddenly suspicious.

"How can she prove it?" several people at once said. "They've taken away her passport."

This seemed merely to consolidate the doubt. "*Prove!*" he insisted, going peasant-stubborn. I might have been caught deliberately tricking him.

On my bag, still stuck to it, was a "Queen Elizabeth" label, and I said, pointing, "Ship — from America."

He squatted down and for some moments peered at the label — again with that blind intensity of the baffled. "Ship?" he repeated.

"Yes, from America."

Another moment or two passed; then all was well. He was beaming once more — unable, one judged, to deny himself acceptance of so dazzling a windfall. His American a real one! Here, right here! He kept on staring, shaking his head; and I wished I could say, "Brother, if it seems strange to you, you ought to know how it seems to me!"

Then, abruptly, he was making a gesture: a flamboyant swing, taking in the whole air. "Soon," he pronounced, in his makeshift German, "soon the sky — all Russian planes! No American! All Russian!" It was said without malice; it didn't even, to my ear, have a bellicose sound but was rather as a small boy, off among strangers, might proclaim, "My father is bigger than your father!"

"All Russian!" he boasted, beaming away.

And suddenly someone in the room said, "No!"

It exploded into the quietness, the single word — with such vehemence, such a passion of repudiation, that we all turned, startled, to see who had spoken. The young wife had turned too, with a frightened look. The face of the husband, the childrens' father, was an ordinary sort of face, thin, ineffectual one would have said, but marked, at that moment, by something hazardous — something not wanted; recoiled from sharply: for in an instant it was as if the others had disassociated themselves from it.

The Russian, halted, wore a puzzled air. Then his face went shrewd. Clattering across the room, he planted himself deliberately in front of them both. "All Russian," he repeated; and stood there, waiting.

The young wife, with a quick, winglike movement, had thrown her arm across the sleeping children. Imploringly, without speaking, she looked at her husband.

"All Russian!" insisted the boy in his long gray coat. His voice was grim, even menacing.

The silence held; it tautened in the room. *Speak! Don't speak!* — which did one mean?

Then quietly, bitterly the young man said, "All Russian."

There was something like a breath admittedly relaxed; the air resettled; and it was then that I became aware of the other girl — the one farther off, seated by herself: shabby, exhausted-looking, but with a patrician face, fine-boned, one had noticed, and still held with a semblance of pride, even arrogance. She was watching me speculatively, sardonically it

seemed. And it was as if she were saying across the silence:
"Now you can see! You so positive, so easily and righteously
judging the rest of us, telling us from your ignorance what we
ought to have done! Now you're experiencing what we long
ago learned. Now you can see how simple it is!"

And it was as if she were saying further, with retaliatory
pointedness, "We perceive that you sit here just as we sit —
doing nothing too!"

I almost said, "Yes!" wanting her to know that something
was acknowledged: that one question personally I had never
asked since the right to ask it had yet to be proved. "Why,
under the Nazis, didn't you rise up? Why didn't you risk for
yourselves — and your families — the concentration camp,
the torture chamber, the gas oven, the pit? Why didn't you
act?" There are those in the world (and some of them are
Germans) who have earned the right to ask such a question;
I am not one of them; and so I do not ask it.

But the question behind, the prior question — that was the
one. Crucial, inescapable, among strangers or friends, everywhere and incessantly in the broken cities, in the villages with
their bells and geese and "Grüss Gott's," even in the mountains and meadows and woods, it was as if the words ghostily
spoke themselves: How did it happen? how come to pass?
Why was it that in a country not "backward," not "barbarous," a civilized country, Christianized, as culturally mature
as any on earth — among the people of Bach and Luther and
Kant, of Kleist and Goethe and Beethoven and Hölderlin —
so evil a thing could reach absolute power?

I wanted to say, "Yes, the result I can grasp: doing nothing
in the face of the accomplished fact. But that other — the
allowing of it to come to pass — " There was the question
that posed itself.

The Russian was relaxed again. Amiably, interestedly (the incident apparently in a moment forgotten) he was leaning over and peering at the sleeping children. Patting their heads, he said something sociably in his own language; then, "Name?" he demanded, turning to the mother. Her voice was just audible: "Willi, Gerda." He repeated the words, teaching them to himself. The children lay limp and curled as kittens; and, "Willi?" he asked, indicating the tumble of yellow hair. "No, Gerda," she told him, in the same tight voice. He unbuttoned his coat then and dived into a pocket; he was rummaging for something, a photograph, it proved. Handing it to her, he stooped close and looked too. "Little brother — little sister — " he was pointing out; and he spoke their names, "Kolya, Nastya — " Rigidly, as if ordered to, she held the picture; one waited for her to say something; but nothing came; and after a minute or two, with a brusque gesture, he took back the photograph, and straightened himself again: looking, as he stood there in his ungainly long coat, suddenly separate and far from his own with nobody to admire his little sister and little brother.

He left the room after that. Clattering out past the police. And now one of the two unobtrusive men, sitting together on the bench opposite, said to me in English, "If you Americans had listened to us Germans this wouldn't have happened, is it not so?"

It was the opening gambit in a familiar game. I had learned, by now, just what to expect.

"In what way do you mean?" I asked, as usual.

He made a gesture implying the obvious. "As soon as you defeated Hitler you should have destroyed Stalin. There was your mistake."

"In 1945, I suppose you mean?"

"Then you should have acted. The Russian armies you could have destroyed at that time. Everyone knows that."

"But at that time the Russian armies had just helped to defeat Hitler. We were — if you remember — allies in the fight."

"That was your mistake. To believe it possible to have such an ally."

"But surely the choice was yours, not ours! You made us allies. By attacking Russia."

"We attacked because we understood the nature of the danger."

"We?" I said. "The German people? — not Hitler?"

"In respect to Russia, Hitler saw the danger."

"Then you attacked willingly?"

"We were forced to take action against a world menace."

"And was Poland a world menace, and France, and England?"

He said quickly, "I was never a Nazi. Many wrongs were made."

"Including," I suggested, "the pact with Russia?"

"We were forced to protect ourselves, in order that we could act."

Even in broad daylight one could feel a blurring out: a kind of miasmic mist enveloping one.

I thought back to the end of the war — the European end: the exact day.

San Francisco in chalky, sunlit tiers above a glitter of water ringed by hills that were gilt against blue in the bright May air. The British, all standing, toasting the King; the Frenchman with tears in his eyes, and my Czech friend saying, "At last! at last!" — her home, her family, suddenly within reach. The Greeks and Dutch and Yugoslavs and Danes; the robed

Saudi Arabians and South Africans with old Smuts and Nor-
wegians and New Zealanders and Lebanese and Turks; and
Mr. Gromyko, in the ballroom of the St. Francis, saying with
a smile, "Try the red caviar — " as Natalia Sergeyeva, vigorous, and casual in her tan beret, called out, "Now you can
come to Moscow!" where, she had promised, I should meet
the writers, her particular friends: for we had talked earlier of
how the poets of a country could time and again be an inmost
pulse so that one touched, in touching them, denominators
primary and common to us all. "Germany Collapses!" "War
Over in Europe!" The words a great blaze, a fanfare through
the air; and the sense of one's fellow men walking free —
Regina, too; and Friedl, and Klaus: through country after
country the doors flung wide, the lost voices lifted, the hands
outstretched. . . .

On that fine spring day, all lit with sun.

"In 1945," I said, "the United Nations had just been
created. And you think it possible that the American people
— or any people, anywhere, if it comes to that — could suddenly have turned and done such a thing? Attacked a country
that for four years had been desperately fighting the same
enemy?"

"It is the difference," said the man, "between the long view
and the short one."

This, too, I had heard before; and it was, by now, more than
could be stomached. "Or the difference," I said, "between
doing nothing and doing, positively, one thing at a time! Who
was the world danger in 1939? Who invaded and terrorized
all Europe? Russia or Germany? We acted against the evil
that was the immediate evil. And presumably — if you
weren't a Nazi yourself — you're grateful that we did."

"Please," he said, "yes, that is so. But to be delivered from

Hitler, only to find Stalin has been put in his place — "

"Stalin isn't in Bonn. I've just come from there," I said; and almost added, "Far from it!" thinking of Bonn. But the words we were speaking seemed suddenly useless, shadowy and fugitive; a spectral exchange. Where could one start? In such a wilderness of errors.

One of the police had stepped into the room. He tramped up and down, noisily but without point. Someone asked him, "When does it come, the train?" and he said, "Later," in a hostile way, so that nothing further was tried conversationally. The night inched along. It was growing colder now. And in the dismal dimness we looked a sorry lot. Huddled on benches. All held the same way — but at variance; without fellowship; each sunk in his own plight. Friedl and I, sitting close for warmth, were reading the several posters pasted on the walls. Statements like "Unity, Freedom, Reconstruction!" — "The Dollar is a Great Power but of Far Greater Power is the Strength of the Simple People When it Is under the Leadership of a Party that is Guided by the Teachings of Marx, Lenin, and Stalin." Later on I was to see posters in full, raw force; but these seemed impersonal, aridly academic, like formulas issued from a distant schoolroom.

Only Siegfried had remained active. Having finished his sausage he was now, with an effect of inexhaustible energy, mending a broken strap on his bag. The roof could cave in — or his whole world (as it had) — and there he would be, still going strong. And I was back for a moment on a Californian road, with cypresses against the sea and a great slope blue with lupine: coming down by myself through the flood of flowers with a copy of Rilke's *Letters* in my pocket, and meeting, without warning, as they came the other way, a company of young men — being marched along: erect, still tanned by a stronger sun and with a vigor that cut steel-like through the easy air. Prisoners of war. From the Afrika Corps.

They had marched past as if lords of the earth.

A mouse skimmed suddenly across the floor. It darted this way and that, with lank lengths of tail; and I jerked up my feet, as I always do. But at once several people (among them the elderly woman, touched to life) exclaimed, "A mouse!" sounding pleased, affectionate.

The first note of warmth! The first thing *shared!*

And one thought — where on earth! except in Germany! Feeling a kind of violent exasperation. All the postcards one remembered — with little fawns and birds: mailed by people who had cried "Our Führer!" And one remembered, too, the stories to be heard here time and again. Like the one about the eagle, which was true, Friedl said; and alas, why not? as both parable and fact.

At the close of the war, so this story went, a whole village was waiting eagerly to be liberated by the Americans. (This was something, of course, to which one soon grew accustomed: the presentation of a Germany "occupied" by the Nazis — of a people "victimized" in essentially the same way as were the Czechs, the Dutch, the French, etc., and therefore equally and logically dependent upon a saving force from somewhere outside.) So here were these villagers, simple folk, fed up with Hitlerism, heart-sick of war, greeting the conquerors with open arms. Freedom had come to them! Democracy had arrived! All were longing to renounce what had been. "Help us! show us!" was the attitude of mind — as high overhead in the spring-bright sky the great bird splendidly and silently soared. For above this village, on a craggy height, for time untold an eagle had nested. It "belonged" to the village — "unser Adler." Cherished by all, from child to hoaryhead, it hatched out its young; it brooded nobly; sunward it struck to cast upon the fields the flying shadow of its untamed wings. And a few days after the Americans had come, early one morning, a G.I. went out and "just for fun" shot the eagle.

And that whole village, the story went, was so shaken to the core by the barbarity of the deed, so irrevocably shocked, that all hope and faith were instantly destroyed. "We expected good men, enlightened and wise; we were told they were bringing us a better way of life — and instead they are men who for no reason at all have killed our bird, leaving the young ones to die in their nest!"

The first time I was told it, I said, "What a rotten shame!" The third time, I said, "I'm glad it wasn't a child." "A child?" "Yes, or six million Jews. Or even just all the males of a village — against a wall."

And I looked, now, around this desolate room: very cold, dead tired, and frightened, I suppose, too. Why was one here? Among these people? It wasn't incredulity but a kind of recoil. "This benighted race!" had said the Englishman on the train; and friends had said, "Germany? but why Germany?" With Paris gala again, and Switzerland full of comfort, and Italy with its endless entrancements for the eye — with almost anywhere else, it seemed, a preferable place. One sat here among those who a few years ago were believing what? were behaving how? and who would today, if the tide hadn't turned, be who knew where? with the gun in *their* hand.

Suddenly one felt hopelessly lost in it all. In this mystery of a people neither primitive nor negligible who had proved, so many of them, at some point in their mentality, as vulnerable as a savage in twilit jungle to monsters and myths. All the paradoxes seemed to whirl in the air. The anarchic romanticism — the scientific exactness; the superb sense of history (as a formalized study) and the disastrous inability to assess history in the making; the sensibility, often so quiveringly exquisite, to every nuance of one's own suffering with the *will to be unaware* of the sufferings of others. The flowing lyricism — and the iron heel; the isolation of the ego with the longing to belong; and that urge to grasp so enormous a thing, the answers to a whole universe, that the immediate first step is too picayune to take. . . .

I wanted to stop thinking; to be done with it all. After all, the gun was in other hands! One had spoken smartly enough of the "immediate evil." Well, here it was! Immediate with a vengeance! One had better concentrate on the Russians now. And as for the Germans — repudiate them or accept: a benighted race let it be, or a people come to terms with without a splitting of hairs.

But the desire to understand is a strange desire.
And I thought of Hans.

II

That morning, in the Schloss Nymphenburg, Prince Ferdinand had told us that we ought to go to Prien. He had just finished his breakfast, and on his beard, rather endearingly, there was a soft dot of egg.

We had encountered him crossing one of the glittering baroque rooms — portly, courtly, and looking so nice that on an impulse we said hello (there was no one else about) and found ourselves invited beyond the bounds laid for sightseers into a study facing the magnificent gardens — all fresh-lit, dew-glinting, and unlittered by tourists at this early hour. The study itself was massed with photographs: Bavarian crowned heads, heads coroneted, heads helmeted, with Kaiser-like mustaches and imperious stares still surveying a world grandiosely intact. On a table, framed handsomely and in the place of honor, was another kind of photograph: an American major — looking frank and casual in the highflown company. He was introduced to us, by name. "A very fine man. We grew exceedingly fond of him here in Munich, and greatly regretted his having to leave."

Prince Ferdinand himself, for the tail end of a House, was admirably undecadent. In his seventies, he told us, he was still a practicing physician.

"You are?" we said. "Why, good for you!"

And he approved of us, too, because we were friends.

"An American and a German exploring together, that is a fine thing. It is well that people should see it happening — that you are enjoying yourselves; enjoying each other!"

(This was something, as a matter of fact, a number of times said. The G.I.-Fräulein relationship was different: an inevitable development, anywhere at all; but a friendship, a close one, and particularly one marked by spirited disagreements — in restaurants, we had found, on trains and boats, people watched it interestedly and when, after one of the open bouts, we laughed and went on, the friendship unimpaired, it was as if a rule had been surprisingly broken: a new prospect disclosed.)

In the study, among the photographs, we exchanged quantities of information, as one sometimes does on the spur of the moment, with nothing to go on but the immediacy of a contact; then we stood up again, and with a kind of brisk elegance he kissed our hands. (What thousands of hands in seventy-six years!) "When you've finished it," he invited, "this journey of yours, come back and tell me all about it. And now run along, both of you, to Prien."

In Prien there was another castle, his favorite one, we'd learned, and a professor it would be profitable for us to have a talk with. So back at the station, with our two bags, we said, "Why not?" and leaped just in time onto a starting train; only to find, in due course — with Prien outside but us flashing through it — that we had landed ourselves on the Orient Express, with the next stop, it seemed, in Austria, at Salzburg. There are some adjustments, of course, that could hardly be easier. "*Salzburg!*" we exclaimed. It hadn't been meant. But since such was the case — what a heavenly idea! And there, not very long afterwards, we were.

The usual conglomeration of police swarmed aboard; and it was at this point that again (so familiarly, alas) there was discovered some sort of hitch in my papers. I had, it appeared, in a fashion indecipherable — for it was "impossible" to do so, everyone declared — entered Germany, at Aachen, without having my funds officially recorded in a currency-control book. I didn't even *have* a currency-control book. "What is it?" I asked. This sort of thing is always happening. For there are those who in spite of the most immaculate intentions, all eagerness to abide by the majesty of the law, nevertheless seem constantly to be breaking rules. I am one of them. And each time, when it's out, I turn bright red, as if caught with the loot in full flight. "But what are we to do?" Friedl wanted to know. And it was then that Hans appeared upon the scene.

He was a tall young German, of student age, and candidly delighted to come to the rescue. (Later we were to learn that he was earning money like this, by acting as interpreter for the customs officials, in order to resume studies at the university in Munich.) And in no time at all he had somehow converted the "impossible" offense into an engaging feat.

The Austrian police (exuding more charm than dedication to the law) laughed with what appeared to be purest enjoyment. Little papers were scribbled on; this and that was stamped. All, one gathered, had been wafted into propriety. Then Hans carried our bags for us down onto the platform.

"I do thank you," I said. "And really, you know — I can't think how it happened. They don't think I did it deliberately, do they?"

"Come with me," Hans said, and led us into the office of someone who proved to be in command of the police. An elderly man, hawk-eyed; seasoned; inscrutable. And here, in a quite gratuitous conversation, I received the assurance that it was, without fail, the person who exhibited all the earmarks of guilt — who turned scarlet, trembled, dropped things, even wept — who was adjudged, by this expert, innocent as a lily. "Really?" I said, no end comforted. And Hans declared, "He has examined thousands and thousands of people, for over thirty years. He is a very clever man. It is the eyes he goes by. Each time he orders a body search he is proved right." We looked with great respect at this clever man; and said, "Thank you very much," and came out again.

"And now," Hans asked, "where are you going?"

We hadn't thought of this. "Where should we, do you think?"

"Do you want to stay in the town, or go off in the mountains?"

"Oh, mountains!" we decided; in the same breath. Suddenly it seemed wonderful to be free of ruins. Mountains —

that was it! with cowbells and churchbells and yodeling and Lederhosen, and nothing in sight broken or maimed.

"Meet me here," Hans said, "at seven o'clock. I myself will take you to the best place."

So for the rest of the afternoon we wandered about Salzburg, and sat at a café under trees by the river, with the bridges arching it and the castle above us, drinking hot chocolate all flounced with cream and eating those pastries that for very lightness fly into flakes as they are bitten into. At a table next to us an Englishman, also with chocolate and pastries, observed quizzically, "*Who* was it won that last war?" But I thought of other meals we had had: with refugees crowded miserably together; with workmen in the Ruhr; even with friends. The bowl of boiled potatoes in the middle of the table. While the prosperous (so speedily, and mysteriously, resurrected) feasted at large. "I think I prefer the English way," I said.

At seven o'clock we returned, as arranged; and it was as if Hans were someone for a long time known. "Hello! hello!" we all called out, delighted to remeet. And carrying our bags again, he hustled us onto a gray Special Services bus, otherwise occupied by an assortment of G.I.'s — several of whom (it was at once evident) regarded askance this easy association with a German man: for it's an interesting fact that although the conqueror's consorting with the women of a country is taken for granted, the reverse arrangement can evoke an instinctive resentment.

But here we were; and away we went. Away, that is, until we jerked to a halt in the deepening dusk, and in swarmed all the police again; for we were, it appeared, re-entering Germany. Out came the passports, the permits, and so on; then off once more, with a wild hurtling around curves as if we were being driven, as possibly we were, by an ex-Luftwaffe pilot — with the moon coming up now, glitter-bright, and the dark shapes of mountains thrust everywhere about us. Then it was Berchtesgaden; and here we got off.

We had dinner at an inn. In a low, crowded room: where music was being played, by three men on stools with feathers in their hats, and where people wearing bodices tightly laced and green jackets and Lederhosen and dirndl skirts were now talking, now singing without self-consciousness, sometimes all together, sometimes only a few, and for a little while a girl, very charmingly, by herself. And one thought of how Madame de Staël had written, in 1813: "It has happened to me to enter small cottages blackened by smoke . . . and immediately to hear not only the mistress but the master playing voluntaries on a harpsichord . . . the scholars walk through the streets singing psalms in a chorus." They weren't psalms or voluntaries, but those innocent and melodious little songs that seem to belong half in a child's nursery and half on a mountain in sun and wind. Everyone in the room looked tanned and relaxed, as if all day he had been vigorously climbing; there was simplicity, and gaiety, and a kind of gentleness too; there was nothing except what they were creating themselves.

And one thought of the recreation centers and the requisitioned hotels, where the Americans were to be found: the juke boxes and comic strips and Bingo Tonight; the Hollywood films. . . .

Hans had wolfed down his Wiener Schnitzel. So rapidly that we said, "Let's have some more," and ordered it for him; realizing now that he was thin as well as lean and that this sort of meal occurred none too often. And gradually, over the table, with the music going on, he told us about himself, and especially about that which lay closest to his heart: his desire to "understand" the world outside, England, France, but most of all America.

Nearly every student with whom we had talked had, of course, said the same thing. Nearly all of them had spoken longingly as if from a closed room. To get away, to "catch up" with everybody else — it was the primary theme, constantly harped upon; but Hans went on to say something more. He wanted to get away, true, like the rest; but the desire was a pointed one, fixed to a purpose. He wanted to experience what he had never known in order to bring back what he found to Germany.

"Already," he said, "there is a little I have learned. I was in Czechoslovakia — "

"You were?" we said.

"My eyesight is not good, not for the Army, and so they sent me to work in a factory there, and I met many people from other countries — Dutchmen, and a Norwegian boy, and my friend Henri."

It was a moment before I grasped the implication of the words: why "many people from other countries" had been there.

"During the war, Hans?"

"Yes, during the war. I met those people, and we talked together, and Henri became my friend. Whenever we could find books we gave them to each other; he knew many books. And he taught me to speak French — that is why I can be an interpreter like this."

"And did you teach him German?"

"No. He spoke only French." And he went on, without hesitating, "It is good, is it not, to have such friends? That is what I believe. And when German people speak in that other way, about the French, I say, 'No, it isn't true! They are not all bad.' And I tell them about Henri; I tell it many times."

The irony had touched neither his voice nor his mind. Telling the Germans, who had invaded France, that the French people were not "all bad"!

But there is a difference between the deliberate mental trick, the contortionist maneuver to evade facts, and the ignorance of a Hans. All his life he had lived in a twisted world; and this health of friendship he had found for himself. No one could have helped him, there in the factory; he had reached out; this far he had come.

"And now," he said, "I will tell you my dream."

It was something, clearly, not often told. He leaned forward, and it all came with a rush — his dream of one day starting a school.

"Because our education is still bad, still wrong. You know that?" he asked me; and I thought of the roomful of students at Stuttgart. We had been talking about the poetry of T. S. Eliot and someone, at a point I was taking issue with, had pronounced, "But Professor X says so." "I don't care if he does; I still think it's a silly idea," I had said (never having heard of Professor X anyhow); and it had been, in the silence, as if one had up and thumbed one's nose at Holy Writ.

"Yes," Hans said, when I spoke of this. "And much more, too. And it must be changed, I think, by us, ourselves. And to begin with it must be a little school — " Words like a chime, one realized suddenly! The awareness, the willingness to conceive of a first step: the acceptance of gradations, stages, a process.

"Oh, Hans, yes! do start a little school!"

"It is good, is it not?"

"It couldn't be better!"

And he told us then how he had been studying American

history and literature with a professor whose exceptional work in Munich we had already heard about. "Not many people understand him," Hans said. "There aren't many people in Germany, you know, one can talk with like this. Germans," and he added, "or Americans either."

"Have you talked with many Americans, Hans?"

"I should like to," he said, "but they do not seem to read these books I have found. It is difficult to understand. Or perhaps they do not wish to talk about them with me."

The old loneliness: time and again evident. And one thought of the young German women too, the exploratory ones (so separated, it seemed: so needing to be assured of the existence of one another) who had grasped our hands, who had said to us as we left, "If only this could have happened earlier! If only there were others who would share their ideas!" One thought of Erika walking beside the Rhine. "I love them, you understand, my husband and child — but there is something more in me. You know what I mean. But if I speak of it here I am looked at as if I were wrong in the head. Why aren't there people one can talk with like this?" Americans, she had meant. "But Erika, there *are*. Just look at them all!" "They live," she had said, "in a world of their own."

"In this school," Hans told us, "you know what it must be? Not just books, but learning from the way that things are done." And he took suddenly out of his pocket a thick notebook, meticulously written in. "Listen!" he said, and finding a certain page in it he read aloud: "Inaction is cowardice, but there can be no scholar without an heroic mind. . . . He who puts forth his total strength in fit actions has the richest return of wisdom. Character is higher than intellect. . . . A great soul will be strong to live, as well as strong to think. Does he lack organ or medium to impart his truths? He can still fall back on this elemental force of living them. This is the total act. Time shall teach him that the scholar loses no hour in which the man lives."

And I was back for a moment in another room, sitting on the floor (there weren't any chairs) with the poet whose work is already to be reckoned with in the world of poetry. Leaning against his books, I had glanced over my shoulder and found myself smack against Emily Dickinson. "Why, Emily!" I had said — strangely moved: for what a bold flight across time and space, from the Amherst garden to this city of ruins. "You know her?" he had asked. "But of course I do!" And he had said, "Let each of us read one aloud." And I had read, for the book itself opened to it —

> Success is counted sweetest
> By those who ne'er succeed.
> To comprehend a nectar
> Requires sorest need.
>
> Not one of all the purple host
> Who took the flag today
> Can tell the definition,
> So clear, of victory
>
> As he, defeated, dying,
> On whose forbidden ear
> The distant strains of triumph
> Break, agonized and clear.

And he had read another; and we had talked for a long time — with such congeniality, with so much to share, that at one point we had laughed, and reached out and touched hands, until (it was Eliot we were speaking of now: a recurrent theme in such conversations) I had asked, "And what of his social views? His political position?" There had been a sudden break in the flow. He had said, after a moment, "Eliot is a poet." "But he's a citizen, too. He votes, doesn't he?" It had been as if he were having to rescue me from a lapse: "The poet is concerned with the timeless verities. He speaks for what eternally is." "But the verities, aren't they implicit everywhere? Surely timelessness doesn't exempt one from now." "Emily," he had said, "has been dead for a long while, but here we've sat, reading what she wrote. Suppose she had written of the squabbles in her street — " And he had gone on: "There will always be those in league with the immediate, who serve the fact at the expense of the truth. We have had such poets, here in Germany. As they have them in Russia. Or in any country. And such a one betrays not only himself, and the calling of poetry, but his hour as well. For in seeing only his hour — what can he bring to it?" Several times this had happened, in talking with Germans, and I never seemed quick enough to anticipate and forestall it: finding myself assigned, in some peculiar way, to a position I'd never dream of occupying. "But good heaven, of course not! I recognize that! The point is, Eliot *votes!* He's a man, a citizen, as well as a poet. As all of us are. Whatever we do — " But suddenly one had known that here we were apart. This man, this poet, vital and courageous and dedicated and incorruptible (for all of this one perceived him to be) would suffer, perhaps, if it came to the test, the final penalty for his poet's faith. But he had delegated to others — to the rest of the group — responsibility for a world in which he might speak.

Hans said, "That was written by an American. Ralph Walter Emerson is his name."

"Waldo," I corrected.

"Please?" he said. I spelled it, and carefully he rewrote the word. Then, "You know him?" he asked, eager, delighted.

"Sometimes," I said, "I've wished that an airplane could fly over Germany and drop thousands of copies of *The American Scholar*." And Friedl told him, "I used it at our Amerika Haus. All winter, in every class."

Hans looked as if he were ringed with shining cohorts. "You see!" he exclaimed, "we are friends! It is so!" And diving into his book again, "Listen," he urged, and read: "The power which is at once spring and regulator in all efforts of reform, is the conviction that there is an infinite worthiness in man which will appear at the call of worth, and that all particular reforms are the removing of some impediment . . . not by the men or the material the statesman uses, but by men transfigured and raised above themselves by the power of principles."

"That," he said, "is what I must understand. The principles that he means. Then I think we will know — " He hesitated, as if seeking to shape into words something still at an under-level of thought. " — how to act," he went on, "how to be brave. At the right time, and in the right way."

He spoke, I think, beyond what he saw. In his desire to see.

After that he told us of the different things he had read: Whitman and Lincoln and Stephen Vincent Benét, and of the men he had learned about and thought about to himself, Jefferson, Garrison — "and John Brown," he said. Which was why, having missed the next bus we were to take, we found ourselves sitting on our bags beside the road, singing for Hans "John Brown's Body." "Again, please!" he kept on saying; and away we sang, there in Berchtesgaden, until he had memorized the words of the song and was singing them too.

Eventually another bus came along; and after riding for some distance we got off again. The bus hurtled on; we were alone in the huge night.

"Now we must walk," Hans announced; and when a German says walk, walk he means! We followed him as he strode across a small bridge, with the black glitter of a river underneath; then between pointed trees and after that out onto a slope with the great moony heights upflung all about us. It was cold and brilliant and totally still. It was splendid beyond words, but, as we climbed, Hans began saying words aloud. They rang out on the immensities of air, familiar and yet somehow different, or deepened, so that it was as if for the first time, here in the heart of the Bavarian Alps, one was hearing them the way they were meant to be heard: not a fixed dogma, an oration with drums, but disclosure and discovery and affirmation:

"We hold these truths to be self-evident, that all men are created equal: that they are endowed by their Creator with certain inalienable rights; that among these — "

Hans climbed in the moonlight, leading the way.

" — all experience has shown that mankind are more disposed to suffer while evils are sufferable than to right themselves by abolishing the forms to which they are accustomed. But when a long train of abuses and usurpations, pursuing invariably the same object, evinces a desire to reduce them under an absolute despotism, it is their right, it is their duty, to throw off such a government — " He had learned all of it, to the very end. "And for the support of this Declaration, with a firm reliance on the protection of Divine Providence, we mutually pledge to each other our lives, our fortune, and our sacred honor."

And he went on, after that: "Four score and seven years ago our fathers brought forth on this continent a new nation, conceived in liberty and dedicated to the proposition that all men are created equal. Now we are engaged in a great civil war —"

He broke off and said, "You say it, too!" So we joined voices, speaking together the Gettysburg words. " — testing whether this nation, or any nation, so conceived and so dedicated, can long endure —" What one had forgotten, or never learned by heart, Hans remembered: having come to it by himself and with no time to forget. "We cannot dedicate, we cannot consecrate, we cannot hallow this ground. The brave men, living and dead, who struggled here, have consecrated it far above our poor power to add or detract. The world will little note nor long remember what we say here but it can never forget what they did here. It is for us, the living, rather, to be dedicated to the unfinished work . . . to the great task remaining before us — that from these honored dead we take increased devotion to that cause for which they here gave the last full measure of devotion — that we here highly resolve that these dead shall not have died in vain, that this nation, under God, shall have a new birth of freedom, and that government of the people, by the people, and for the people shall not perish from the earth."

In the mountains, in the moonlight, the words rang out.

"He spoke for everywhere, did he not?" Hans asked.

We reached, then, the inn he was taking us to — where he lived himself through these summer months: a long, low shape from a story-book with its carved wooden balconies overhead and light in a sudden yellow stream from the door. He said, simply, as he led us in, "I have brought two friends — " and Frau von Engelmann took us into her arms, as if we were daughters, and had been expected; and going to sleep in deep feather beds, in a big room opening on to the dazzlement of the night, it was as if we had intended all the time to come here, and had arrived when we should, and were happy and safe.

In the morning we heard our names being called. "Friedl! Dorili!"

And going out on to the balcony that belonged to our room we found Hans standing below, about to leave for his Salzburg bus.

"Look!" he said, throwing out his arm; and he asked eagerly, "Do you like it? Is it good?"

We looked and looked. All morning at our feet. There lay the wide and parklike meadows, still gilded with wild-flowers and crisscrossed by paths along which moved gently, like figures in a frieze, the full-skirted women, the men in Lederhosen, the children with little satchels strapped to their backs — practicing yodeling in their thin clear voices as schoolchildren elsewhere might practice their sums. There were cowbells and churchbells and goat bells as well. There were steep mountain pastures, as one lifted one's eyes, with the dark fir trees and the white glint of houses. And, above all, there were the mountains themselves: the great rocky masses, powerful and yet in this blue and gold air so ethe-realized that they might have been dreamed upon the sky.

It was Eden; Arcadia; it was like a Psalm made plain. It was just as one would plan to have the earth.

"Oh, Hans!" we said.

"It was right, yes?"

"It couldn't — anywhere — be more beautiful!"

He again made a gesture: pointing far up now. "Can you see it?" he asked.

We tilted our heads. And immensely high above us, in the topmost airs, there was something — just a flash, just an inkling — discernible. Somehow the eye found it in that radiant blaze. Suddenly one knew, without being told.

We stood silent, all looking up. The Eagle's Nest. The pitched-into-the-heavens madness of a myth. There was nothing to say, until Hans said, "He is gone! we are here!" as if shouldering with the words the inescapable task.

As he crossed the meadows in the morning light, we could hear him whistling his new tune.

111

SEVERAL OF US MUST HAVE slouched off to sleep, for we were starting up suddenly and asking, "*What is it?*" Through the silence of the night had come the sound of a train. It roared closer; it was here; it had slowed to a halt. There was some sort of commotion immediately outside; and we all pressed avidly against the three small panes, seeing, in the darkness, a swarm of figures and there, just beyond them — O beautiful sight! — the lemony glow of lighted windows.

The Berlin train! Headed the other way!

"Remain! be seated!" we found ourselves told. So we all sat down again, but in different places. Orders were being militantly shouted back and forth; everywhere the stomping was revived full force. Then, just as suddenly, the air went quiet; there was no sound outside, nothing to be seen. The inspection of the train had started, one assumed.

Three police had been left with us in the room. But all at once they seemed negligible. One hardly noticed them. We might have been passengers in any station, normally preparing to resume a journey. The children, roused and stood on their feet, leaned wobbly and rosy against their parents' knees while their hair was combed, their short coats straightened. Things taken out of bags were being thrust in again; straps were fastened, and all the familiar little gestures made, the assemblings, the tidyings, the making sure.

Outside, within hailing distance, were other people! Real people, like ourselves! no longer were we alone! And the fact seemed to work like an alchemy within the group so that we were loosed into talking back and forth, consulting one another and comparing dilemmas.

The problem, now, was how best to manage: how to get in touch with relatives and friends, and to borrow money (as several must do) in order to return to the places started from. Nobody was in a position to help anybody else. Nobody had any real information either. Siegfried, still authoritative, still splendidly in trim, looking fed, fresh, and as if the whole stopover had been arranged at his request for some purpose of his own, stated, "We'll be taken to the first station across the border; it will take us an hour." The girl in the raincoat (she had sat down next to us) asked, "Where are we to be returned to — Frankfurt?" speaking across him as if he hadn't spoken; and one of the police said, "Yes, Frankfurt."

He had been strolling about the room; and for a moment he seemed to hesitate there in front of us. The other two guards, talking together, were further away, over by the door. The Volkspolizei. Booted, with their guns. He moved off again; but suddenly, in that moment, one had become aware of him.

In another few minutes he had strolled back. It was expertly done; nobody seemed to notice. He didn't quite look at Friedl or me, and when he spoke it was softly, without change of expression.

"How are things in the West? Is it the way they tell us it is?"

In an instant, warningly, the girl shook her head. She had gone cold, guarded-looking; and the young man, turning on her, rapidly said, "I am not a spy!"

The exchange flashed out, almost between moments.

And again I was left lagging — startled, unprepared. For again here it was, the unexperienced thing. These people had been conditioned to secrecy and treachery, to strategies and techniques one had never known.

He stood there, motionless; and I found myself staring hard at his face. Was he one who had been here all the time, or had he only now come into the room? It was impossible to tell. Although aggressively confronting us throughout these hours, they had all, one realized, been lumped together; a de-personalized force; no one of them had been *seen.*

He turned then; and as his eyes for that moment straightly met one's own it was as if he were deliberately exposing himself to an appraisal. A curious moment. For which of us was on trial? A young face, not unsensitive: not brutalized, certainly; not matched, one would have said, to the role he was cast in. There it was; and if much, or everything, depended upon a decision — how would one decide? In what way act? It was his word, proofless, against the weight of the circumstances; in a way, against the whole weight of our hour. A face, a voice, a handful of words. How many times, and in what agonies of uncertainty, had people — with no more than this to go on — been forced to choose? To risk or not risk; to live or to die?

I stared at his face, trying to tell; and realized now that everything that had ever happened to me, the whole shape of my life, made it natural to believe, alien to suspect. A man adjudged innocent until proved guilty. It was the very backbone of attitude and conduct in one's world. There was even that further commitment to a conviction: better to err in judgment and be oneself betrayed than falsely to indict another man.

It was as if one were pitched into a different country of the mind. Suddenly shaken. For could one, here, be allowed such scruples? Mightn't they belong to a privileged air, a kind of ethical luxury, like all the other luxuries? "Better oneself to be betrayed — " But where did oneself begin and end when each touched another at every turn?

"No man is an island — " and all the rest of it: one had grown up listening to and accepting such words. They were part of one's tradition, communicated in the nursery; basic to a Christian concept of the world. But they had meant, always, something affirmative. And something simple (or so it seemed now) with expanded awarenesses matched logically to action. Because no man was an island, because all were intermeshed, one took sides, spoke out, acknowledging in both personal and public affairs the responsibilities incurred by a positive conviction. But here, to be aware — what did it mean? The father corrupted by the children who must be spared. The prudent many imperiled by the insubordinate few. And I thought of Ilse — haunted by the question that nobody had understood. "But was it right? Should I have done so?" Nobody had understood; for she was a "heroine," she had behaved under the Nazi occupation as everyone in the room (we were Americans, the rest of us, at a Harvard party) could only blindly trust that he would behave himself if faced by the same challenge.

She had been in the Danish underground — a girl gently bred; rather fragile to look at and not much older than her student hosts, but in some part of herself aged into another dimension. "How does one know? You forget that I undertook to act for others. I didn't say to them, 'Do you wish me to do these things?' I assumed that right, and the right to implicate those who did nothing. To everyone who spoke to me I was a germ of danger. I was serving my own conscience — but at whose expense? Who gave me the right to appoint myself to that sort of role?" There had been in the room a kind of awkwardness: a sense of disrupted, even violated, assumptions. Somebody (a college girl "taking" political science) had said sturdily, as if sticking to a truism, "But you were *wonderful!* Of course you were! It's people like you — " And Ilse, speaking patiently, as one speaks a language imperfectly understood by those addressed, had told us then about her father: how he had been taken among a group of hostages and how word had been conveyed to her in another part of the country that unless she gave herself up to the Gestapo, by a certain date he would be executed with the others. Because she was a "heroine" something still had been assumed. Nobody had spoken; and she had said, still patiently, from that knowledge within herself, "You see, it was not his life or mine. It was many others as well. It wasn't death one feared. It was not knowing if one could stand what came before death. I had never suffered physical pain; I didn't know if I could be trusted. It was my father's life against the other lives I might betray." And she had said then, with a kind of tiredness, "For you, here, it is all so simple! The words you use, the things you believe. Everything is written in big plain letters — that is wrong, this is right — like a child's book. You have 'loyalty tests' — 'loyalty oaths,' as if one could promise like a child to be good. But loyalty to what? What do your words mean? The men who started your country were 'disloyal' — and Socrates, and the Christians defying Rome. If you knew what loyalty is, you would know the answers. You would be able to tell me, if you knew that, whether I killed my father or saved my friends."

Another country of the mind — the new country, perhaps: for didn't it await all of us, wherever we were? The ambiguities, the moral hazards, the old certainties dissolved. Not simple any more. Not a child's book of truisms. "For God and So On!" "For Such-and-Such a Way of Life!" Whole pages of words, once slogan-plain — how were they to be read in this harsh shift of air? Two and two made four, in one zone or another; fire burned, water froze, the apple fell. But when it came to how a man should stand and act —

The guard, without looking at us, was indicating something: the label on my bag, I suddenly realized. He said, still speaking expressionlessly into the air, "I would like to go there. I would like to see what it's like outside." And he asked again, "Please — how is it? Is there much unemployment? Is there enough food?"

When Friedl said, "It's not as they tell you it is; you can be sure of that!" the girl next to us abruptly got up. She walked away. And there leaped into his face, at the repudiating move, a look so explicit that I found myself saying, "I believe you!" — saying it positively; because I did; it was the truth.

And with the words came a curious sensation of relief. So

it went like this! At the actual point. If one had to decide, one decided; that was all!

"But *why?* Why are you working for them?" For there was the gun, strapped to his back; and if one of us were suddenly to make a dash outside —

He didn't answer for a moment; and when he did it was more by gesture than by words. "How can I make you understand?" he asked.

The familiar helplessness. The plight — and the plea. The malady at the core, it time and again seemed. Not only behind a line, in this hireling guise; not only in Germany (although in Germany the malady was at its deepest and most complex); but to be found, too, in how many quarters — in the French salon, in the villa in Italy; at the café, the university, the studio, the home. The concept of man caught helplessly between forces. Man as victim; man acted upon. And one heard Giuseppe beside the Arno saying, "If I am asked 'Will you stand and fight?' I must say I don't know, for I've not found what it is I should be fighting for. And will it matter, anyhow, to those of us in-between? Whichever of you wins — if there's a war — we're the ones who'll be destroyed; whatever we do." And Dirk saying, "If I speak from cowardice, there is my conscience also!" Dirk who was nineteen; and Claude, older, the civilized man, with his sensibility and taste (and his scrupulous dedication to what he called "spiritual" values and I would call "cultural" ones), Claude saying, "You are fortunate in perceiving such a choice. Since to many of us, I'm afraid, there exists no David. From where we stand we see only two Goliaths."

He had moved off, the young man with his gun; and some minutes later, with the same show of casualness, one of the other two guards was standing there.

Having spoken, this one proved readier to communicate.
"You write for a newspaper, don't you?" he asked; and added,
surprisingly, with a sudden grin, "I'd like to see what you'll
write about this!"

Evidently my passport had been deciphered by someone;
and so we enquired about it; could I have it back?

"Yes, when you leave. Don't worry, it's all right.'

We asked him then about the Russian soldier; and he said,
"Ivan? Oh, he's a good fellow. He doesn't want to be here
either." And the other one, the inspector? we wanted to
know; but he didn't answer that. Instead, with a nod towards
the elderly woman (looking white, worn out, but sitting bolt
upright with her furled umbrella and neatly darned gloves) he
said quickly, "Tell her not to go back to Heidelberg. Tell her
to get off at Bebra, across the border, and find somebody with
a typewriter who'll put the date on for her. The same kind of
typewriter — it must look the same. Then tell her to come
back in another two days."

"But the Russian — won't he notice?"

"He'll look for the date; it's the date that matters."

He was saying something else; then stopped short; and one
realized that the third guard, posted by the door, was staring
over at us curiously. "Thank you," Friedl said, speaking into
the air; and I said it after her, carefully not looking at him —
feeling like a child beginning to catch on; learning the ropes.
And feeling, too, something that was almost pleasure in the
recognition of a threat! The spasm of distrust, quick and
sharp — somehow it was reassuring; even bracing. A proof, it
seemed, of accuracy of instinct, of one's capacity to reject as
well as accept, so that I would have liked to draw attention to
the fact; to say, "See, I'm not being taken in! I can dis-
criminate! I can recognize an enemy too!"

(For how haunting, how crippling this contemporary fear — not so much of being deceived as of appearing deceivable! With compassion, hope, all the intuitiveness of the heart, shriveled before the dread of being labeled "soft.")

"That one, by the door," I was saying to Friedl, "we must be careful of him — " when suddenly everybody jerked to attention.

There was a sound outside. The engine, starting up. And coming back through the darkness, with a stomping of boots —

In the same instant we were all on our feet.

"*Our train!*" someone cried.

And as it happened it was as if one had known that it would. Even with the outflare of panic in the room, with people shouting, "Our train! you're letting it go!" and one's own voice, as shrill as any of the others, crying out, "Our train! our train is leaving — " It was as if one had known all the time that it would leave, so that everything we were now doing was no more than a performance, a prescribed set of antics almost tediously being gone through. Thus people behaved, when caught in such a way — and we all moved forward, in a small surge, as the guard at the door shouted at us, "Halt! Go back!" Even the gun, suddenly in his hand, seemed a matter of routine. A gun — to be sure. And now another guard, a fourth one, coming in from outside, was commanding above the uproar, "Quiet, everybody! Everybody be seated!" We all stood where we were, holding our bags. "What's wrong? What's the matter? Why are we being held?" He announced authoritatively, as if reading from an order, that "there hadn't been time" to put us on the train. "You must remain. You must wait." "How long?" we all cried. "Four hours — five — " But he had hesitated at that. With the command delivered, his knowledge was at an end. And again there was that sense of being pitched in a vacuum, with no focal point, no one to appeal to. And no one it was the slightest use beating against with fists.

Just as suddenly as we had all stormed up, we were silenced. Everyone wore the same kind of outstrained look. We were listening — as off it went into the night, the sound of it growing fainter, fainter, on the air. Not a soul on the train had been seen or heard; and none of them, those passengers headed for the West, had known that here — a few yards away — were eleven of us. But one found oneself overwhelmed by a sense of loss. As personal and acute as if we were being parted from invaluable friends. They were gone, gone! One strained to hold on to the last faint hint of them. Then there was nothing. We were left behind.

We all sat down again. With relief, it almost seemed. As if a pantomime of protest had been scrupulously run through.

And now began an orderly, discreet little exodus, conducted with such decorum that it was hardly to be associated with a common urgency. The father went first, holding a child close to him at either side. He said something to a guard, and was escorted from the room. Minutes later he returned; and next — getting up and being taken out — was the elderly woman, carrying purse and umbrella, as if bound for church; then the two quiet men, buttoned into their overcoats; then Siegfried — striding forth and in no time at all striding back into our midst, with the invigorated air of one who had bolted up and down the Matterhorn. Friedl and I stuck it out to the last; then we, too, were conducted from the room and down a short passageway, dimly lit.

The two guards accompanying us (by chance or not) were those we had spoken with.

"Don't worry!" they said quickly. "It will be all right."

"Is there anything we ought to *do?* The Russian? — " we asked; but this was disregarded. "Don't worry," they said again.

There seemed suddenly a thousand questions crowding up in one's head (months later, with Ernst, the questions were to be asked) but another door was being opened, at the end of the passage. "Please," they were saying, as if ushering us into a conservatory; and out we stepped. Into total blankness.

The night was enormous — pitch-black and dead still.

The guards, remaining stationed in the open doorway, turned on their flashlights to make a little path; and we walked out along it, side by side. For a moment or two there was the feeling that if the light were stepped from we would plunge into space; it was like a narrow plank. Then the ground became solid, like any other ground. Gritty, winter-brittle, with weeds and grass — somehow it seemed astounding! The ordinariness of it! Russian Zone ground: ground Behind-the-Curtain! But just the same, now it was trodden on, as anywhere at all; and there, far above us — that was the same too; for a silvering of stars could be faintly caught. We were still in the world! We were still *here!*

We walked on, keeping close, for several yards.

"When do we *stop?*" I suddenly asked.

And all at once we began to laugh. There was no holding ourselves. There we stood, simply helpless with laughter. Turning around, we called out, "Where? How far?" And the guards, we realized, were laughing too. It was like a sudden break into normality, into health. "Anywhere!" they were calling back. "The field is yours!" The little lights beamed out, still fixing us in their line; and we made exaggerated gestures, waving our arms — "Turn them off! Go away!" The torches disappeared. In the entrance we could just make out two figures, their backs turned.

The night was complete now. And somehow, closed about us, it seemed less ominous: we were standing in a field, under a starry sky —

"Ought we to make a run for it?" I wanted to know. And again we were shaken into helplessness by the laughter. If we were to make a run for it — trust us! notoriously bereft of a sense of direction! Like homing pigeons we'd doubtless head for Poland or Czechoslovakia!

We took another few steps, holding hands; we stopped; then stood again. Not a thing could be seen. It was piercingly cold, and the stillness was absolute.

"How far in do you suppose we are?"

But there was no way of telling. Somewhere, close at hand or miles from here, a line was drawn. It couldn't be discerned, even by day; a bird in flight wouldn't know where it was, or a leaf blowing across it, or the winds themselves. A line like a myth, in the minds of men. And here were we, inadvertently behind it. With immensities of space out there in the dark: country beyond country, going on and on, with people by the million, the tens of millions — all out there literally; all teemingly alive; each one of them as real as we were real, as *feeling*, as *caring*. . . .

One stared into the night. One said, aloud, "Millions and millions of people are there!"

But it was too much to grasp; too gigantic a fact. It was like reading in a newspaper of astronomical casualties. Famine struck; war raged; but the child who was starving and the man pitched forward, the anguished old woman beside the smouldering home — how faceless and voiceless, how abstracted they were: without blood or stink or writhing or curse. How safely sterilized into statistics on a page. One little girl could be lost in a Maine wood, and half a nation was touched to personal concern. There was her picture. She had a name, and parents (understandably distraught), and was wearing a pink dress and carrying a toy. She was a real little girl; and when she was found people said to one another at the grocery counter and the bus stop, "Debby's been found! Isn't it wonderful!" Tons of print. A deliberate sensationalizing of a family's fright. And yet something else, too; surely more than that. For in spite of all the mawkishness, and the promoted sales, wasn't there implicit in the concern called-forth evidence of the potential scope of the heart? A million children were hungry and endangered and forlorn; but they couldn't be realized, not on such a scale; and so one child, fastened upon, was cared about and shared. "She's safe!" people said, as if she were their own. But the others, all the shadowy multitudes out there —

How could they be grasped? As the actualities they were. Czechs and Hungarians and Russians and Poles, half a Germany full of Germans and incalculably more than this — all the swarms and hordes of people on earth — how could they possibly be taken in?

And for a moment the old despair flooded up. As if *man* were lost in the multiplicity of men.

When we went inside again, back to the room, everything all at once seemed extraordinarily reassuring! The dismal light was translated into a genial brightness; stark benches had a hospitable look — sofas they might have been; and there was even (just at first) the illusion of warmth! So must the tent feel, to the jungle explorer, or the security of the igloo in Arctic wastes. But it was the people, the nine of them looking up as we came in — it was the people who mattered.

For how movingly consequential they suddenly appeared! Like relatives returned to; not chosen friends, but kin, all bound together at a level below choice. Nine people, or eleven of us, at a nameless point. Not heroic or exalted or remarkable in any way. Quite ordinary people. Even less creditable perhaps than the average, with our falterings and insufficiencies laid all too glaringly bare this night. And yet *mattering* — that was the transcendent fact. If we were generals and cabinet ministers and scientists, the fact would be acknowledged, and our disappearance from a train would result in a deafening confirmation of our "importance." But we weren't. We were us. Quite ordinary people. And if we were never to be heard of again we would be grieved for certainly by those who loved us (the pregnant daughter in Berlin, the children's grandparents) but there would be in the world no yawning gap; no tide would be turned; everything would go on. Not more than a handful of other human beings would even know that once we had walked the earth.

And yet each of us mattered! There the fact blazed. For either it was everyone, or no one at all. Surely in the end it must come to that. For the differences and distinctions — how inchling they were! measured against the stupendous magnitude of a universe. In that final infinity of time and space, that dimension of being unframed by flesh, either all men must matter — in some absolute way — or none of us at all; not any; not one.

Now through the windows there was a gradual thinning of the dark.

It was that coldest of hours: dreary and drizzly, with the dawn bringing only a dead pallor to the air. The elderly woman had begun to cough; she seemed to have shrunk, and even Siegfried looked finally drained of energy. When we spoke to the guard it was the first sound made in the room for a long time. Wasn't there, we asked, anywhere we could go? Couldn't the children and the old lady at any rate be warmed? They stood there, the police, conferring for several moments; some sort of argument appeared to be going on; then, "Come," one of them said; and we all got stiffly and hastily to our feet.

At the door Friedl and I were told to remain. The others were taken off somewhere down the corridor, and we waited, feeling abandoned, until two of the guards returned — the familiar ones again, we recognized with relief. "Please," they said, inviting us to come; and we found ourselves back in the room where we had started, where all of us had stood (a thousand hours ago) herded together, dazed and shouting.

Two chairs were placed for us in front of an iron stove, and someone began building up the meager fire. We sat down, hunched forward, with our hands held out. "The others — " we asked; and were told, "Don't worry, they're being looked after." Several other police were congregated in the room; and with their guns taken off and stacked against a wall they looked shabby, unofficial, in the dispirited dawn, with a sudden awkwardness, one felt, interjected between them. It was as if no one quite knew, in front of all the rest, what attitude to allow himself, how relaxed to be with us. The fire blazed up; and the young man who had been attending to it straightened himself again. "It feels good, yes?" "It feels *wonderful!*" we said gratefully. And it was then that we noticed there was a telephone behind the desk, and asked if it would be possible to get word to Berlin. Our friends would be meeting the train at eight o'clock; couldn't we at least let them know we were safe? Unfortunately, we were told, it was against the rules:

the telephone was used only for "official business." "Too bad," someone said, and sounded as if he meant it. Another of them, at the desk, was now opening a drawer; he held something up. "You see, it's safe!" It was my passport, I realized; and at the sight of it I felt almost lightheadedly pleased. "Isn't it funny," I said, "about a passport! When it's gone, I mean. You feel as if you'd lost your nose or your liver!" Everybody laughed. And the next thing that occurred to us was the tin of cocoa.

It was packed in one of the bags, and was intended for Regina. "If you'll bring some water, in a saucepan," Friedl said, "we'll make cocoa for us all — " But at that point there was an abrupt stopping short in the atmosphere. A woman guard had come in. Muscular, unsmiling, glancing at us with hostility, she unslung her gun and stacked it with the others. She strode out again. And it was one of those moments when one felt an instinctive, half guilty relief at being left with men, even men who were police — since there is, in the face of a de-womanized woman, no familiar way out: neither a lax falling back on feminine appeal nor a sisterly rapprochement. Someone went off then, and returned in a few minutes with a saucepanful of water. It was put on the stove; the sweetened cocoa was found. "And a spoon," we now called for, becoming bossily domestic. There was a spoon too, and half a dozen thick mugs. The room was becoming eased into a normal sort of room. Here we had stood, all shrilly crying out. And now there was a fire, and a pot being stirred, and a blond boy fingering the "Queen Elizabeth" label. "Is it a big ship?" he wanted to know. "Too big," I said. "You hardly know you're on a ship — " and I found myself adding, "Come on a smaller one, if you come!" "If we come," he said, "we must grow wings, like birds!" Three of them were standing there;

they all laughed, in the same way. And then we noticed that another guard was using the telephone. He was speaking carefully into the mouthpiece, saying something about Berlin. Over his shoulder he asked us, "If it is possible — what is your friend's name? What sector does he live in?" We gave him Klaus's name and the British sector address. He turned back, speaking softly to whoever it was —

And it was then, at that point, as there we all were, pouring cocoa into the mugs and beginning to talk, that the sound came from outside. The sound of a train.

Friedl and I stopped short.

Nobody spoke.

But suddenly it was as if a decision projected itself. There was no consultation; no sign that one could see. But, "Quick!" came the word. "This way! Quick!"

Our bags were snatched up, and I found the passport in my hand. "*Quick! Quick!*" — the same word used before, but not shouted at us now, with no stomping of boots; and we were out in the corridor, being raced along, and now out of the building in a bitter drizzle of rain. There was nothing to be seen but the train itself, already grinding to a pause across the cindery ground; and racing towards it with the guards we suddenly called out, "But the others! Where are the others — ?" then saw they were coming too, in a disorderly scramble as if flying for their lives. Everything was urgent, chaotic, unexplained. There was no more shapeliness to the denouement than to the start. "Where will it take us? Where are we going?" "Across the border," we were told. "Bebra," someone said; and someone else said, "Don't let them see your passport! don't speak English — " A compartment door was opened and we were thrust inside, unfooted for a moment among a crowd of boots. Workmen were sitting there, peering blankly, saying nothing. As the door was slammed the train began to move, with the others, farther back, still getting themselves aboard — the children passed up like leggy little bundles; Siegfried leaping goatlike; all of us on.

We hung side by side out of the open window. On the ground, in the rain, stood the little group of guards; and, "Thank you, thank you, *thank you!*" we called.

Their arms were lifted; they were waving in return. "Auf Wiedersehen!" they called back to us as the train gathered speed.

"Danke schön! Danke schon! Auf Wiedersehen!"

The red star behind them had blurred into the air; the five figures were faceless, were dissolving as we waved. They were lost, but for another moment the voices were still heard.

"Auf   Wiedersehen — Auf   Wiedersehen — "   Coming through the mist.

IV

That was the first time I headed for Berlin.

And I didn't, then, make a fresh start, but went back with Friedl to her Hessian home.

It was late afternoon; the day had cleared, and we walked on cobblestones in a cackle of geese through the dense and complex and rooted thing that the simplest of villages anywhere is. We walked quietly through it, carrying our bags, and then out into the open under an immense flow of sky — into a lovely candor of long-sloped hills. Everything had a silvery shine to it in the sun; it looked clear and free, with the fields all reaped and the oak trees, belonging to legend and song, crowning the bare undulations of earth.

It was warm enough for us to have coffee and cakes on the balcony. We sat there chattering, terrifically wide-awake, for one felt keyed up to that precarious kind of buoyancy in which everything in one's head, the whole of life, seems about to break into the most sparkling lucidity. Friedl's mother kept filling our cups and plates. Her father asked question after exploring question — the gentle schoolmaster who had sought to stem a dark tide in the red-roofed village lying storylike below. The baron, a neighbor, came over to extend greetings. He said, at once, "You were more than fortunate! You must never do such a thing again! I wouldn't dream of traveling to Berlin myself." He had just, it appeared, returned from Spain, where his family had certain business investments. "Now in Spain," he said, "one is safe anywhere. Franco knows how to keep a country in order." And when Friedl, referring to the road beside the house, a narrow road winding from this village to the next, said, "The whole Seventh Army passed along here — " the baron observed, "Ah, yes, to be sure, what a day that was! We were sitting at dinner, there we were and suddenly," he lightly gestured with his cup, "suddenly American soldiers burst into the room! Pointing their guns at us! As if," he said, and he sounded urbane, and genuinely amused, "as if my old mother, my aunt and myself were dangerous enemies!"

One could see them elegantly looking up at the intrusion. And the uncouth Americans, straight from war —

All at once the delayed tiredness struck like a blow.

When at last I woke up another day had begun.

There was the sound of church bells, melodious across fields, and all the comfortable sounds that come rightly with the earth, a child's voice in the garden, a bird singing in the sky; the faint cacophony of village cocks and geese. I had slept, I found, more than fourteen hours. I'd been clean knocked out — novice that I was. Only a small thing had happened. We had been taken off a train. No harm had come to us; we'd been roofed, and even helped. In a world full of melodrama it was the merest incident, and to be shaken by it like this — how untried one was. How unlettered in the hazards and excruciating tests that not only are experienced by millions of people but times without number are triumphantly survived.

And suddenly I was overwhelmed by the miracle of that survival: by the fact that there exists, in ordinary men, that which can withstand what bone and nerve and even the uttermost strength of will could surely, of themselves, never endure. I thought of my friend Madeleine, who had been with the Maquis: who had known capture, and rape, and the unspeakable degradation of those final infamous months at Ravensbrück. When German was spoken she still involuntarily winced; but the project she was working on she herself had devised — the bringing of German orphans for a holiday into France and, in exchange, French orphans taken into German homes. "To prove what, Madeleine?" "To prove I belong positively to life," she had said. And I thought of Eduard, the university student, who, at fourteen, had seen his Czech home burned and his father hung, and had said, "For three years I knew nothing but hate; then someone said to me, 'They've destroyed you too!'" He had spoken to a roomful of other students, not afraid to use words like "God" and "redemption" and "faith" and "love"; and whatever was thought of the terms themselves, or of the particular form of belief he had found, it was clear that he spoke from an inner health; that he was not destroyed. It was clear he, too, belonged positively to life.

And lying there like that, in a Hessian village, with the sounds of morning crystalline on the air, I felt something I had never quite felt before, or not consciously, not explicitly, as I felt it now.

It was a leap of gratitude for all the courage in the world.

The courage to be found at this, our own hour, but far beyond that — the immemorial blaze of it clean through time: from all the dungeons and arenas and gallows and stakes, before mob and tribunal and on bloody fields and at the lonely, forever-besieged outposts of thought. One thought of all the deeds from the beginning of time (even a young father for a single moment saying "*No!*") that like strokes of light have hewn for us through the dark whatever footing we share, whatever certainty of direction. Old Socrates lifting his hemlock cup. The prophets, the heroes; and all the nameless, the unnumbered, the unknown-about men — facing sword and beast and lash and screw at whatever inquisitional hour was theirs. With the singing high in the consuming flame. With the truth, rung out, safe in a universe before stopped in the throat.

One thought of them, and suddenly it seemed a great thing: to be walking the earth with one's fellow man.

JOURNEY BEYOND A LINE

Turning and turning in the widening gyre
The falcon cannot hear the falconer;
Things fall apart; the center cannot hold;
Mere anarchy is loosed upon the world,
The blood-dimmed tide is loosed, and everywhere
The ceremony of innocence is drowned;
The best lack all conviction, while the worst
Are full of passionate intensity. . . .

W. B. YEATS

Our doubts are traitors,
And make us lose the good we oft might win,
By fearing to attempt.

SHAKESPEARE

Creon: Know'st thou the edicts which forbade these things?
Antigone: I knew them. Could I fail? Full clear they were.
Creon: And thou did'st dare to disobey these laws?
Antigone: Yes, for it was not Zeus who gave them forth,
Nor Justice, dwelling with the Gods below,
Who traced these laws for all the sons of men;
Nor did I deem thy edicts strong enough,
That thou, a mortal man, should'st over-pass
The unwritten laws of God that know not change.
They are not of today nor yesterday,
But live forever, nor can man assign
When first they sprang to being.

SOPHOCLES

Fellow citizens we cannot escape history.

The dogmas of the quiet past are inadequate to the
stormy present. The occasion is piled high with
difficulty, and we must rise with the occasion.
As our cause is new, so must we think anew and act
anew. We must disenthrall ourselves. . . .

ABRAHAM LINCOLN

journey Beyond a line

WHEN NEXT I started off for Berlin I managed to get there. As a matter of fact, I got there rather more intimately than I'd bargained for!

This time we were driving. And this time there were three of us.

Stephen, in London, had bought a little English car; and Rod, having completed a fellowship year at Trinity, had come over from Dublin to join the expedition. Crossing the Channel, we landed on a golden midsummer afternoon in Holland, at The Hook — with that incomparable feeling of having a whole continent, or the better part of one anyhow, all there before us: all the cities and landscapes and patterns of life; the songs that are sung and the dances out of time; Chartres and Salzburg and the Dalmation coast, windmills and mountain edelweiss and the lions of Venice. All Europe before us! In a brilliance of sun.

The first evening we spent drinking hot chocolate with friends, at a café beside the moonstruck sea at Scheveningen. When German spies first began infiltrating the region, the

75

Dutch police, we were told, used to ask suspects to pronounce Scheveningen! The inescapable reminder — still hovering in the air. A violence called "the Germans" had broken darkly out: they had marched these streets, patrolled this very shore; they had ordered the chopping down, for winter firewood, of all the trees in the gardens behind my hostess's home. Everybody, laughing and at ease in this group, knew personally what it was like to be "invaded." And there were other people, people not here — For something suddenly was echoing in my head: something I had been told about the year before. *Scheveningen Prison.* Yes, that was it. The place in which political prisoners had been held, and in which had been found, at the end of the war, torture instruments more ingenious than those of the Inquisition. Here patriots had been condemned; here had died, without breaking under their terrible ordeal, a group of British agents, including women — betrayed (as even his own comrades had been) by Christian Lindemans, that hero of the Dutch Interior Forces, who treacherously had come to terms one day in Brussels with Giskes, head of German Intelligence.

Behind walls perhaps close to where we now sat people had died. In a manner not conceivable in any state of sanity. And they had died — why? For what reason, what point? So that we and our friends might sit like this, on a cool summer evening drinking chocolate beside the sea? So that we might again go holidaying across Europe: looking at the Van Goghs, crossing the Ponte Vecchio? Appreciating the proportions of a temple on a hill. . . .

On that first evening, returned to a continent, I found myself thinking with a queer intensity, "I want something to happen! I want to get closer than I did before. To learn; to understand; to be of more use." To deserve being here, perhaps one meant.

A few nights afterwards we were in another house, outside Amsterdam.

Before breakfast we picked raspberries in the garden with our host. In the raspberry bushes, for some thirty-six hours, the son of the family, then a leader in the Resistance, had lain hidden while the Germans watched for his return. And as his father spoke of this I thought of Ursula. Ursula, a young artist I know in Munich (doing work that is marked by a kind of lyrical innocence) who had said to me when I admired the reproductions on her wall, "The originals are in Amsterdam. I went to stay there, you know, with my cousin Wilhelm — the one who was a colonel; and we had the most beautiful time that spring. Never had I seen such wonderful pictures!" "Amsterdam?" I had repeated. "But when — how?" and she had said, "In the spring of 1943." And I remembered, because of that, the Frenchman at Harvard a year or two ago, and how, before leaving for the United States, he had spent, he told us, the last three days slowly paying his respects to everything in Paris that he cherished most. "It was a pilgrimage of farewell. In case something happens to it before I return." "Nothing happened to it last time!" someone had observed; and he had said, "That was last time. For the Germans there is one thing, at any rate, to be said. They may shoot you, and even make lampshades of your flesh, but for French culture they have a serious regard." And there was Karl, doubly tempered, since he had experienced in the violent shift of our times both a German and a Russian concentration camp. "In Russia it was primitive — full of hardship and chaos, with men dying from the lack of food and care. In the

German camp, for that first year anyhow, there were flower beds at the entrance. And to be found sleeping with lice was a moral offense." He had added sardonically, "Of course, on one's way to a crematorium possibly it's a great pleasure to see a flower! We have, we Germans, such a penchant for the artistic!"

We picked raspberries, and ate them in a sunny Dutch garden. And everything had so glittering and gala a look, was so summertime-rich and morning-bright, that it was difficult to credit winter or darkness or storm.

"Does it all," I asked, "seem far away now?"

"Only as far as the frontier," said our host.

That same afternoon we crossed the frontier.

It was Germany again. But we didn't immediately head for Berlin. Instead, because I wanted to see what had happened to him, we went to Bremen, to look up Peter.

Peter is an American; and for the past eleven months he had been working with the International Refugee Organization, at Camp Grohn, as director of one of the affiliated agencies. When last we had seen him he had been a copy boy on a newspaper. And since I was the one who had encouraged him to resign — and take off for Europe, which his heart was set on — I was somewhat concerned with the vindication of a hunch! One would hardly make a practice of distributing such advice, since to bolt into the blue can be a tricky business; but there are times when something spontaneously leaps forth, and I had found myself saying without the slightest hesitation, "If I were you, Peter, I'd go; I'd do it."

Someone else had said, "They'll make mincemeat of him!" And for a moment there had been a qualm — for that naïve enthusiasm, that ardent concern for the more specialized and dramatic plights of humanity, how could they survive (let alone carry weight) in the seasoned airs of a world where the very vocabulary of hope is suspect?

The answer, of course, was that obviously they couldn't. Not in that first fine flush of innocency. But there had been something more; or so I had believed. For Peter had been equipped with two articles of faith that can, I think, bear within themselves the safeguards necessary for their own survival. He believed, genuinely — and with a matter-of-fact humility none too common — that he had as much to learn from any man on earth as he had to give; and he believed that the primary force in society (no matter how complex, massive and entrenched the counter arguments and evidence may be) is the principle of love.

When he said this, flatly, in so many words, one had wanted to protest, "Oh, please, don't say it!" Well knowing with how deadly a thud they can fall, such highfalutin sentiments — left as words. But this he would learn. That had seemed the point. For what he was looking for, I had felt at the time, was a crucible more exacting than his present experience in which to test the validity of what he believed. That he was giving up a conventional toehold of security, a fixed mode of advancement, and all the comfortable little props afforded by the "familiar," had seemed, I suppose, as immaterial to me as it had to him. For there are those who from the start are somehow concerned, not with "a living," but with life itself. And if this is how they are shaped, then it's best, I think, that they move free; that the risks be taken. Even the risk — and it is a high one — of embitterment.

And so off Peter had gone. With no professional equipment, no advantageous contacts, or money to speak of, and no guarantee of any job ahead. He had simply gone; and to Germany because it had seemed to him that there, of all places,

the challenges were the most acute, perhaps the most consequential.

That had been eighteen months ago. And here he now was.

We found him in a sprawling and swarming camp: an
evacuation point that meant, for the thousands of refugees
coming to it, the end of one life, the beginning of another.
Instead of sharpening pencils and filling inkwells, he had an
office of his own and a staff of Lithuanians and Poles and
Czechs, themselves each waiting for official clearance, and of
young German volunteers; all working together. There appeared to be a minimum of equipment in the place; and everything going on had a kind of fluent, impromptu look to it,
neither professional nor amateur, but rather as if tactics were
being freshly devised at the point of constantly evolving needs.
There was the informality apt to mark any sort of front line;
and at the same time Peter was recognizably at the head. The
Estonian professor seeking some sort of adjustment (elderly,
mannerly, with that raceless look of the scholar who would go
to his death for a footnote in a thesis) addressed him with
respect — the young American in command. The woman
from Krakow, in unaccountable tears; the experienced New
York welfare worker, from an adjacent agency, with an inter-
locking problem; the Silesian couple, demanding "Herr
Direktor" — the whole procession of interruptions involved
decision, action, direct responsibility. Before it had been news
copy carried into a composing room; now it was the very tissue
of other people's lives.

The telephone rang, from Munich; then Wiesbaden; and
Peter, after some sort of disorderly harangue, slammed down
the receiver. He looked first stormy, then utterly sunk.

He said (we had been talking as best we could), "I don't
know the answers any more. I've learned plenty — I'm a dif-

ferent person, I guess. My contract's up in another six weeks,
and I'm quitting then. Somebody else can figure it out!" And
he asked, "What do you do with human nature? Nobody gets
around to teaching us that. We Americans, we haven't started
to think things through. We're all full of slogans and gadgets
and know-how, and telling other people how to re-arrange
their lives — and we don't know them, and we don't know
ourselves, and so we make a mess of things — or the same old
deals under a new bunch of names. Just watch them, these
Europeans," he said, "when somebody starts sounding off
about 'democracy'! Or the brotherhood of man, and all the
rest of the stuff. They know we're coasting on our fancy
words. They know we'll do the same things everybody else
does — and some of them better, like getting drunk and taking girls — only we've got to make it sound as if we're doing
it in church! We've got to believe we're *good* while we're
being *smart*. We're brought up that way. It's the American
creed — "

And he said, veering around, as if out to wallop everything
in sight, "Look at me here! What do I do? I get one answer
going, and it falls to pieces. So I dream up another one. And
the same thing happens? Or somebody thinks it's going to cost
some money! And who's ready, in America, to spend money
on ideas? For everything else, sure — but *ideas* — not us! We
can liberate whole countries with tanks and bombs, but what
have we learned about liberating a man's mind? Look at the
money the Russians spend. They start with the minds. They
know where it counts. And what do we do? We start with
the results. We come charging in telling everybody how
wrong they are because we can't figure out — when it's needed
— what's right. Look at us all here, here at Grohn. What're
we doing? Picking up the pieces. Clearing away the wreckage,

to make room for — what? What comes next?"

And he was veering again, saying, "See that man, the one with the scarf?" (A window was beside us.) "He escaped from the Russians, from Lithuania. He's a doctor, and he did just fine in Germany, because doctors were needed and all he wanted was to be safe and comfortable — and successful of course. Which was okay. Who doesn't? Except that it happened to be 1941, and he was being safe and successful under Hitler's Reich. Then the Russians came again — he was in Königsberg — and there was no more Reich, and after that he didn't seem to make out so well. So now he's got his papers; he's going to America. And how're you going to figure out things like that? Whose side was he on, anyway? What's he think he's *for* — ?"

"And the Germans, Peter?"

For it was Germany he had chosen: it was here he had come to test himself.

"The *Germans!*" he said. And this, from his vehemence, might have been the end! The ultimate frustration. As if we were locked in disagreement, he said, "I'll tell you one thing. If we don't get *them* straight, the rest won't matter! You go to France — to Italy — " he spoke as if they were suburbs at the end of a trolley-line — "you talk with the people, anywhere you go; then you come back here. And you know it's *here* something's going to be settled!"

"Yes," I said, "I believe that too."

For already there was the feeling one had each time: that here, inescapably, for good or ill, were energies and urges — irrational, inchoate, dynamic, semi-mystical — for which neither clericalism nor the humanism of the elite can provide an answer. Or a bulwark either.

"You feel it every time," Peter said. "It's why if we've

failed here — we've really failed. You can't plow under a
people like this. Not these!" And he sounded as if he'd wring
their necks if he could! "So you've got to understand them —
what else is there to do? And the thing is, they want to be
understood. It's what they *need*. Even," he said, "to understand one another, so they'll stop forever trying to gang themselves up — into something phony, like a Race, or a Volk.
Anybody can see why they keep doing that! Because they
don't feel they matter enough, one by one. By themselves,
they think 'Who understands me?' If they say 'We Germans'
they feel all right! And I'll tell you," he said, "another thing.
You can be honest with them. You can talk tough! as tough
as you've got to — if they know you're not just kicking them
in the teeth, not *blaming* them, but trying to figure things out.
And they can tell, too! Maybe people always can. Maybe
that's something else we've got to learn — that human beings
are pretty smart, they can feel what you mean. And if they
think — "

Someone else had come into the room: a fair-haired German girl, one of those on his staff.

All the children, she reported, couldn't go. What was to
be done?

"What d'you mean — they can't go?"

The three buses, she explained, wouldn't hold them all.

Peter said instantly, "They've got to hold them!" He was
up, off, hurtling from the room.

I stood at another window, looking out. There were the
buses, bulging, in a row. And there on the ground, a small
leftover swarm of little children, all surrounding and anxiously
gazing up at a young American, talking his head off: arranging,
rearranging —

I asked the German girl, "Where are they going?"

"To a circus," she said. "They've never seen a cricus. Peter thought of it."

She had come over to the window and was looking out too.

"What sort of a job has he done here?" I asked.

"Job?" she repeated. Then she simply said, "Everyone in this camp wishes Peter were his own brother."

We were taken later on into a small crowded room, where perhaps forty people, seated on benches, were listening intently to a worn-faced, dark-eyed Latvian woman who was patiently rehearsing them in English phrases. They sat there immobile, their gaze fixed on her as she spoke. Slowly, obediently, they shaped the words: old people and young ones, all mixed together; men looking as if they might be peasant and professor, mechanic and artist and physician and mayor; aged women with shawled heads; mothers, girls: all simplified to a kind of vulnerable childlikeness, because all — however meager or rich their pasts — stood again at a beginning, carrying only themselves. "If you are lost, and must tell what you are, what will you say?" the teacher asked. And together, slowly and falteringly, they said, "I — am — a — displaced — person — "

Rod turned suddenly. He asked, "Can you use me? I want to help." And for the following eight days we saw very little of him, as in classrooms like this he taught English to such people and answered questions about the America to which many of them were going.

We were taken into another makeshift building; and here, in a room that was an improvised chapel — neat as a pin, with candles and a few (rather awful!) pictures — a Russian Orthodox priest with his skirts tucked about him was kneeling and scrubbing the bare boards. He turned, looking up over a shoulder, as we entered. He was bearded, with a frank and vivid face: with a look so untroubled, so stripped clear, that he might have been found anywhere at all, at the lordliest of altars, in an open field. "Hullo!" he said to Peter, buoyantly, in English. "Come in, my friend — "

A priest on his knees, scrubbing a floor.

We were taken next into a community room, where, in a semicircle and at first speechless — drinking coffee out of mugs and munching cakes — were a group of the older refugees. It was a "party," conducted weekly ("Peter thought of it") in order that they, the elderly ones, might, in meeting and airing their anxieties, be assured that others of their own age were also embarking upon this new life. Several of the camp officials were there, to ease out diffidences and encourage questions; and everything that was said was at once translated into the necessary languages, so that all might participate in whatever came up. The Polish woman, encountered earlier in the day, was the only Pole present; each time she avidly waited for her turn, and everyone sat silent while she received at last — with nods, exclamations and gestures that dramatized the most humdrum item — whatever the piece of information was. Several times, through her interpreter, she reassured someone else. "The ship is a fine ship, fast and safe. My son already he has gone and he tells me." A postcard from her son was passed around: the Empire State Building — looking wildly improbable! "Ah, ja, ja!" a few knowing ones said. "New York!" Others seemed unnerved. What stupendousness! What a world! How to encompass it? Although they were skillfully and patiently encouraged, there weren't, one found, a great many questions. It was the younger people who were full of them, wanting to know everything; for these, the grandparents, perhaps there was enough to be grappled with in the fact that they were going far away, never to return.

When the party was over, one of the interpreters brought to me an old woman who throughout the hour hadn't uttered a word. She was shawled, and bowed, with hands that Rembrandt might have composed, gnarled and veined above the slope of full skirt. In her face were ignorance and wisdom all mixed; and her eyes, looking out from the simplicities within, were as blue as field flowers. Humbly she stood there, with her folded hands. With what years of living lying behind! what cradles rocked, and soup pots stirred, and dark earth toiled in faithfully and long. The interpreter said, "She wishes to ask you something." The old woman spoke softly, looking up first at him and then hesitantly at me. "She wishes to know — are there, in America, any old people?"

After a moment I said, "Tell her that in America there are grandmothers and grandfathers, and great-grandparents too, just as there were in her own village. And all of them are a part of our lives too. Tell her — " But what one was saying, I suppose, was, "Oh, America, be kind to her when she comes! Oh, Duluth, Minnesota — " for there she was bound, with a nephew, it seemed, and his immediate family, "an old woman is coming to you, with fear in her heart, and all your gadgets will be only a bewilderment to her, and your speed a savagery, and your bigness too much for her mind to grasp. Receive her gently! Take care of her when she comes! Let her feel that she matters, and belongs, and has a home — "

That evening there was a party of another sort.

The head of one of the affiliated relief agencies, who had been in Germany for the past five years, was leaving now, returning to Washington; and at a long noisy supper table sat a crowd of people — Americans, British, half a dozen European nationalities: all fellow workers here at the camp.

Toasts were drunk; songs were sung — the melodious and haunting songs of this continent; a gift was presented (by Peter, in his element); and although people going away, and the giving of gifts, are familiar enough in any area of affairs there was something here that was somehow different, or so it seemed to me — feeling it, moved by it; for here were people, out beyond race, already constituting in themselves a new kind of society. One looked at them, seeing them in such a way. People from many places and of different ages — all singing (as if it had been learned in the nursery) a song from the Tyrol, and now one from the Ukraine: no one of them making a salary that would be looked at twice by the "realistic," the "ambitious," the "go-getters" of the world; with no security guaranteed, no prestige, no publicity; no predictable prospects or settled center. They lived in the flux of human emergency; in requisitioned houses, in other people's countries. And nobody had ordered them to lead such a life. Of their own free will they had chosen these values: these penalties and compensations, whatever they were.

The Englishwoman next to me suddenly said, "I wonder sometimes if we, all of us, aren't the real displaced persons. Those out there — we pack them off to South America, Australia, the States, and sooner or later they find their bearings; they settle in; they're not apt to move again. But we — do any of us belong anywhere, I wonder? Do we really *want* to? Or aren't we, for whatever the reasons may be, escapists from the very world that we're engaged in helping other people to reach?"

She had, herself, lived in Malaya and the Middle East, and

around half of Europe; she was at home in country after
different country, and knowledgeable at a level as untouched
by the diplomat as by the average tourist. She was at home
anywhere — except, one judged, in Bristol where she had
come from.

"Could I go back there? Could I re-enter that sort of life?"
And she said then, "Look at your friend Peter — " who was
busily bringing in several other people (refugees, one gathered:
two violinists, a pianist, a girl with a flute) and assembling
them by the piano at the other end of the room. Apparently
they all shared only a rudimentary German, for everything was
being done with many gestures and much laughter. We sat
there watching them; and the Englishwoman asked, "Do you
think he'll be satisfied to return to what he left?" And she
asked, too, "Was he particularly good at whatever he was
doing?"

I tried to remember him those months ago: sharpening
pencils and carrying copy. "No, I don't think so; not particularly." As a matter of fact, he had been, hadn't he, a bit
of a nuisance? — disappearing with the pencils and being
found, ages afterwards, lost in conversation with a teletype
operator.

"But here — " she said, and broke off to indicate one of
the violinists: a distinguished-looking man, with the manner
of one hoarding precariously within himself the sound of ap-
plause, the warmth of honors. "A musician like that," the
Englishwoman said, "normally Peter'd listen to him from a
gallery seat; here he provides him with an opportunity to
perform! Here he catches planes for Vienna and Belgrade
as he once caught a bus at the end of his street. He crosses
frontiers as if they were brooks. Even when he feels balked
by everything in sight, he's living creatively — in a state of

keyed-up improvisation. He feels important, not as himself, but, on the contrary, because he must if he's to matter to more than himself. The representative of something. Like a cross between a missionary, with the sacred flame, and an ambassador with extraterritorial rights. And there's the seduction! That sense of a unique status, of a specialized role. The exemption from the ordinary — which we're bored by, or unfitted for, or have failed to come to terms with in an orthodox way."

"He told me," I said, "that he's quitting in six weeks."

"Did he?" she said. And suddenly she laughed.

The music had started; and sitting there (thinking instead of listening) I supposed that in a way she was right enough. People perfectly adjusted to their own environment, their own group-pattern, seldom go careering off into the blue. And this is obviously and indisputably to the good, since a worldful of vagabonds would fly apart. But was it, by a long shot, the end of the matter? Wasn't there another and equal truth, and one as indispensable to the shape of our age? We were, all of us, so haunted today by the psychologists' blueprints, by the myth of a "norm" — so shrewd at diagnosing the misfits, the renegades, the deviating flight. But didn't the world in which we live need, urgently and as never before, the very kind of people assembled in this room? And wouldn't they be needed in increasing numbers for as far ahead as any of us could see?

A world was in convulsions before our very eyes. Something was dying, something else coming to pass. And, in this hazardous and momentous in-between, how necessary the people who could move free, functioning at whatever the crucial points were: identified instinctively, by temperament or sentiment, not with the part but with the momentum of the whole. They were needed — and there was surely no danger of too many of them! Since for every Peter, cutting loose from where he"belonged," there would unfailingly be a thousand other young men constituted and equipped to be the pillars of their society. They, in his role, would be rootless, bereft; he, in theirs, pent up and unspent. And wasn't it to the advantage of everyone concerned that this should be so: the steadfast element and the nomadic light, the depth and the range?

For call them what one will — misfits, eccentrics, the rebels of society; or the explorers, the adventurers, the poets perhaps, translating their impulse into the living act — here they are; here they always have been; and it was surprising in a way, when one came to think of it, that it should be an Englishwoman questioning their validity (except that this gnawing at one's own motives, this ruthless self-doubt, is at every turn the mark of our age) since the British of all people have bred such types, whether it's been an Anna off to Siam or a Lawrence among his tribesmen, a Byron in Greece or Livingstone in the jungle, or Drake or Rhodes or Gertrude Bell, or those men and women, like an outleap of light, heading for the rocky rim of a new world.

They have always been bursting beyond their native bounds. Gallant and rake and builder and apostle. Breezing into barbarous and complicated lands; invading (in a crinoline) outlandish courts; charging poles and peaks and desert sands and all the seas that bare an horizon to the eye. They are old hands, these island English, at going away. But for the American a different tradition has accrued. His has been the country sailed *to*, not *from*. A whole continent of his own has been his to explore, so that the same restlessness and daring and imagination could, until recently, be expressed within the confines of his own frontiers. If he's left, and lingered over-long somewhere else, he has been an "expatriate" not an adventurer! The neurotic, not the robust, individualist it has been assumed is the one who deserts Main Street for a boulevard or a plaza. And doubtless, in the past, there has been in the assumption a degree of truth. For the American at the café, the villa, the bar, the coteries of exquisites and the shaggy escapists (not expanding a part to include the whole but repudiating one culture to romanticize another) — in retrospect they seem a dubious lot, and understandably suspect by the solid citizen.

But the world has taken a giant turn. What could be clearer? And isn't there, now, a new necessity — and with the necessity a new adventure?

For better or for worse, Americans by the thousands must now sail out, beyond their own shores and into everybody's world: technicians, educators, welfare workers, advisers and administrators and information-center officers — for better or for worse, so it must be. East and West, out they must go, and in the service of an idea as momentous perhaps (once it is truly and roundly seen) as that earlier version which steered men's minds. Now the Pilgrim voyage is being reversed. And upon the caliber of the voyagers — Who can tell what depends upon that?

I asked, suddenly, what I had asked before. "And how good is he — Peter — at *this* job, here?"

The Englishwoman didn't immediately answer; then, "He has," she said, "a great deal to learn. He makes mistakes, unnecessary ones — it's an extraordinary mixture of naïveté and percipience! And he wants to settle everything in ten minutes, of course. Or start fresh, as if he stood in Genesis."

I thought for a moment she had given her answer. Then she said, "He brings — to a place like this — an invaluable gift. The faith that we make history, and aren't its victims."

Now the party was over; and the one going away was outside, in a jeep, with Peter and several others piling luggage in after her while the rest of us all leaned from the open windows. A kind of beauty, like a patina, lay on everything. For although the evening was well advanced, it was midsummer and in the north, with an afterglow of gold still haunting the air and the whole sky luminous above the acres of camp — the wooden buildings, makeshift and nondescript, in rows and people strolling quietly in the lighted dust, the shawled old women, the shirt-sleeved men. There was a look of evening tenderness to the scene. And now a song started up again, saying goodbye.

Auf Wiedersehen — Auf Wiedersehen, everyone sang, leaning from the windows, watching a friend go. And the refugees, pausing in their quiet stroll, looked up, listening, so that all of us for that moment seemed held at the point of something immemorial and universal, the fact of farewell. Now the jeep was starting, and everyone began to wave. "*Auf Wiedersehen — Auf Wiedersehen —* " deepened the song, and the fair-haired German girl leaning beside me was crying as she sang and waving, waving, with the American going away turned back, waving too, and the old women standing in their folded shawls and the sky all luminous and the singing fading off like the gold slowly going from the evening air. . . .

We had turned from the windows, back into the room.

"Did you know her very well?" I asked the girl.

"No," she said, "she is not one I have known well. But we are all together here. It hurts when someone leaves." And she said that again, as if it infinitely mattered, "'We are all together."

Eight days later we rang up Berlin.

"Regina! Regina! — we're starting, we're off! We'll be there tonight!"

Her voice came warm and gay across a Zone. *"Berlin —* you will *please* remember it is Berlin! You are not to get lost again. This time you *arrive!"*

"You just stay there. We'll arrive all right!"

And she said at once, "Oh, we Berliners, we expect to stay!"

And so we left Peter, and started off.

11

THE AUTOBAHN SWINGS HIGH and bold and bare, a road to carry armies; but there was only us on it. Backwards and forwards, not another thing in sight. And then it was Helmstedt, the official check point, and one felt a curious contraction of the heart. For here, at this end, were the British and American Military Police and flying together in the sunny air the Union Jack and the Stars and Stripes; then a stretch of space, perhaps twenty yards (peculiarly taut-looking, like a kind of silence) and after that the barrier which divides our world, with a brilliant massing of great red flags.

Somehow, more than all the speeches and print, that mute confrontation of flag by flag, with the blank stretch of highway in between, hit the mind. *The cold war.* Well, here it was.

Our passports and military orders, English on one side, Russian the other, were inspected in the office manned by the Americans. Then instructions were issued to us by a gum-chewing Oklahoman who appeared to have brought himself, by a herculean effort, to concede necessity to all this fol-de-rol. We understood that we were traveling at our own risk? That the check point at the other, the Berlin, end was to be reached within four hours and in not less than two? And that — in the event of any kind of mishap — we were to send back an S O S to this outfit by the first vehicle headed west?

And we were to stop for no one. This was repeated. "You understand? You stop for no one, especially any of them in blue shirts. Unless, of course, they draw their guns on you."

To be sure, we said. Quite grasping the point.

"And only one of you go inside, over there," he wound up. "Keep it simple. The guys confuse easy."

We got back into the car and drove across the space (to whom does it belong, this in-between ground?) and the next barrier was raised for us; we again drew up, and Stephen and Rod, with grudging chivalry — for we all, naturally, wanted to do it — allowed me to go inside with our papers.

Here, behind a desk, was a Russian soldier who glanced at and stamped the Russian side of the orders and entered into a ledger several lines of information. It was all done simply, authoritatively, and in five minutes. Then, with the air of one embroidering a process, he proceeded to investigate Stephen's passport, holding it to begin with upside down, and producing — rather charmingly! — a little repertoire of expressions: casual interest, sudden suspicion, an astute weighing of something, satisfaction at last reached, but only just. Then he examined each of our photographs, while I marveled afresh at how everybody in a passport looks almost without fail like an incipient maniac or a full-blown spy. Suddenly he peeered closer; he put a finger smartly down — on, so it happened, my middle name.

"A-n-n-e?" he pronounced, in an enquiring voice.

"Da, da, that's me. Moi — ich — " And I added hopefully, "Like Anna Karenina." But he was not, alas, a literary man; and I said, "I'm afraid you don't know your Tolstoi, but I do, many of us do, and we like very much the Russians we have read about and very much wish we could know you all properly." He said something, too, in his own language. At any rate it made a sound of conversation in the room. We nodded, smiled. The papers were handed back, and he topped off the encounter with a phrase that I chose to believe meant "Good journey!" "I hope so," I said. "Last time there was a bit of an interruption."

And that concluded that; a third barrier was raised. And we passed under the brilliant flare of flags.

About us as we drove, on either side of the Autobahn, lay a wide sunlit Van Gogh-like landscape, all candid, free-flowing, unwithheld. The grain in pale sheaves, the villages, across fields, ripened-looking, compact, with their dull red roofs and needling spires. Villages right here, almost within hailing distance, and yet, one kept realizing, as unreachable, as forbidden to us, as villages in Tibet. And as we drove it wasn't long before we tumbled to the fact that something ahead of us was about to begin.

For raised against the landscape every few miles, slanted to face the incoming cars, were bright and skillfully executed posters. Posters of young people, children some of them: all linked together and of many races, all laughing, vigorous, garlanded with flowers, in attitudes of camaraderie, of shared endeavor — the white arm thrown across the erect black shoulder, the yellow hand grasped. "Welcome! Welcome! Welcome!" flared the signs. "Peace — Paix — Friede — Pace — " And across the bridges that from time to time spanned the road were blazoned salutations and admonitions. "Berlin Greets the Youth of the World!" "Youth of the World Unite for World Peace!" "Friendship Wins!" "Fraternal Greetings to the Korean Youth!" "Demand the Abolition of the Atomic Bomb!"

Obviously something was about to take place!

And as a matter of fact, we had made it just in time, for the very next day a precautionary ban on all travel to Berlin was imposed for two weeks by the Western Powers. Quite inadvertently, and right on the dot, we were heading into the thick of the *Weltjugendfestspiel* — the Soviet World Youth Festival for Peace.

That evening, in the British Sector, we were in Regina's home.

And everyone at once said, "You couldn't, if you'd tried, have timed it better! Now you'll see the sort of thing that we used to have!"

The tall glass doors stood open to the night, with the balcony beyond high among linden trees; and we all sat there in a circle around the supper table, talking our heads off. Regina herself, chic and gay; and her mother, never met before but immediately saying, "And here is a *Berlin* Tante for you!" — having heard about my Tante collection; and Herr Professor, the uncle visiting from Dresden; and Klaus, still looking the ex-Wehrmacht officer until, knowing him, one saw so clearly something else. Klaus who had been a prisoner-of-war in Russia, for more than five years, and who had returned from the inward mess of that experience (every now and then such men are met) unembittered, straightened out: now committed with courage, like his friend Gerhardt, to a hazardous new role in this Germany of theirs. There we all sat. And as

Tante, white-haired and nimble of wit, spooned onto plates the endless boiled potatoes, it was difficult to credit what one knew to have been so.

(The next morning, as we turned off the Kurfürstendamm, Regina was to pause and point across a street. "It was there, in that cellar, that we all hid. For those days and nights. The Germans were at this end, the Russians down there." Tante had crawled out on her hands and knees to bring back food for them, and water in a pail; and one evening during a lull in that last hopeless fighting, when they had felt that the cellar could no longer be endured, they had climbed, Regina and her sister Johanna, upward into the ruins to a room where a piano was miraculously intact. And there, with Hitler dead in his bunker — although they didn't know that, or anything at all — they had played and sung, Bach, Brahms, as if singing to save their own sanity in the world, and all at once, as they sang, they had realized that German soldiers, exhausted and doomed, were standing there in tears, listening to them. Soon there had been no more fighting outside, because no more Germans; and Tante had hidden both of them under rubbish of some sort, and sat on top of them — that night when the other girls, found and taken off, could be heard through the darkness crying out. "Over there," Regina was to say in the morning; in a sunlit street.)

In bed I lay awake for a long time thinking. This was Berlin. And one saw again the headlines black across newssheets. "Berlin Fallen!" "Berlin in Flames!" When Berlin had been the heart of a deadly foe. What bewilderments it posed, this world of ours! How unreliable the enmities of men! "Here!" one could say — fixing the adversary; and all in a twink it was somewhere else. Darkness and light — what unplaceable stuff!

For a long time I lay there, wide awake.

The next day everyone kept saying the same thing. "Now you'll see something you've never seen before!"

Which was true enough. And fortuitous indeed. The only problem being, as they were obliged to acknowledge, how, under the circumstances, one was to see it!

Already some hundreds of thousands of participants were congregated, it was reported, in the Russian Sector. By the fifth of August, two days ahead, when the opening ceremonies were to take place in the Walter Ulbricht stadium, well over a million of them were expected to be on hand. Regina herself, and the rest of our friends, were hardly in a position to facilitate matters — involved as they all were in press and radio and official activities that made it inadvisable for them even to cross into East Berlin. So we drove out to the Press Club, to ask for advice; and three lounging newsmen, amiable over whiskies, said at once with the easy authority of old hands, "Oh, you don't want to get mixed up in *that* mess. A hell of a time to come to Berlin!" and we drove away again, feeling as if we had slipped in sophistication, until I said, "But I *do!*" Gauche or not! I was bursting to get mixed in it; and obviously if anything was to come to pass — if the event was to be experienced and not merely beheld — it must be up to oneself. Nobody was going to say, "Please, do come!" One would just have to go.

Which was why, the next morning, bright and early, there I was in Potsdamerplatz.

This, of course, is the all-too uneasy heart of Berlin, where three Sectors dramatically meet. And, if one stands there facing east, looking leftward across a wasteland of cleared ruins, one sees a white building, arrestingly intact — and flanked now, for the Festival period, with a brilliant intermingling of the world's flags. Formerly Dr. Goebbels' Informazionsministerium, this was the headquarters of Gerhardt Eisler: the as-yet undeposed chief of propaganda for the Russian Zone, reputed operator of a master spy ring, and at present exercising, it was being said, more power (directly derived from the Politburo) than his predecessor had under the Third Reich.

I stood there looking at it, thoughtful-like. Then I started off.

For it had come all over me in the middle of the night that if one wanted to get into a den, why wouldn't it be politic to consult the chief lion?

The previous evening the three of us had gone exploring across the line. We had dressed ourselves, under critical supervision, in the most nondescript of clothes; we had walked with great tact, and refrained from speaking English, and, on the S-Bahn, had shrunk so modestly among other people that we were barely able to re-find one another. And for the whole time, wherever we went, conversations stopped dead, every eye was riveted on us. We might have been wearing the Crown Jewels, or been announced at each step by a fanfare of trumpets. A sober respect for the fine art of disguise was, in that hour, belatedly conceived. Clearly there's more to it than the novice suspects! And so, this morning, instead of getting myself up to look like a deprived, worse-for-wear Fräulein, it seemed much more sensible to go over frankly, even flagrantly, as oneself — wearing, as a matter of fact, a patchwork cotton skirt that could be seen leagues off and that was to prove throughout Europe (even in the wilds of Yugoslavia where the peasant costumes are spectacular beyond words) a veritable sensation.

The distance between Potsdamerplatz and the Ministry is

not considerable; but it was richly studded with armed Volks-polizei. And since all of them appeared instantly smitten with interest, I said sociably to each one, "Guten Morgen! Infor-mazionsministerium? — " as if presenting an engraved card; and, when Thalmannplatz itself was reached, sailed into the building with the utmost ease, since I suppose it didn't occur to the underlings at the entrance that one would care to enter unless confident of a welcome.

I was, I found, in a big lobby. There was a desk, of great size; a good deal of bareness; and several men present, of the more flintlike type.

"Bitte schön," I said, to the one who appeared chiefest. "I should like to speak with Herr Eisler."

This was something, apparently, that wasn't very often said. At least, not by persons in cotton skirts.

There was a staggered sort of silence. Then, "Why?" I was asked.

"I should like to consult him about something," I said. And sat myself down on a nearby bench.

Several eyes fixed me like pistol shots. There was a coming-together, a whispered consultation (the day was to be sibilant with whispered consultations); then someone made a muted telephone call, and someone else was dispatched across the hall and up the stairs. After that there was a long and uneventful interval, which I utilized profitably by assembling — and in all seriousness, now that I was here — the arguments for my case.

These, it seemed to me, were simple enough. And alto-gether reasonable, if the simplicity was held to. Here I was, fortuitously in Berlin: and here, taking place under one's very nose, was something that would provide an invaluable opportunity to see — in operation — the tactics and techniques of the other side. Here was a campaign to win "The Youth of the World," and here a chance, for the taking, to meet them, talk with them, to learn what they were thinking and why they were thinking it and how explicit or absolute their commitments were.

I hadn't come over as a propagandist. That, it seemed to me, was an essential point. For if I was to ask for courtesy treatment, then, in return, a certain kind of courtesy must be extended. My purpose was to expand my own understanding. Not merely to confirm the evilness of evil, but to perceive more accurately the underlying "why's." What was it that was "appealing," "persuading," "galvanizing"? What hopes, what ideals, what reachings-of-the-heart, common to all of us, were being subtly enlisted and shrewdly shaped to the dark ends of this perverted world?

I had come to look, to listen, to learn. That seemed the sum and substance of the matter.

At which point there smoothly appeared upon the scene someone from a higher level of authority. One knew it at once; one almost stood up. A medium sort of man, impossible to memorize, he had that almost quintessential "ordinariness" which, when encountered under circumstances not ordinary, can somehow be so much more formidable than horns. His manner was civil; and he spoke English.

"May I ask," he enquired (not unreasonably), "what your business is?"

Brass tacks now seemed called for; so I should, I told him, like to attend the opening of the Festival. In fact, I should like to attend all of it; and since I'd been given to understand that this would be impossible without special credentials, I should very much appreciate having such credentials. "Herr Eisler, I'm sure," I pointedly wound up, "would be able to arrange it."

Herr Eisler, I was told, didn't, alas, happen to be at the Ministry that morning.

"Then please," I said, "I should like to see the next most important person."

It was one of those touch-and-go moments, I suppose. The ordinary man remained silent, immobile; then, with a gesture, "Come!" he said, in that good old peremptory German way.

Up a stairway we went, then along several corridors — through a series of doors that opened, then closed again, with a rather excessive amount of click. Looking back over one's shoulder, one saw Volkspolizei. Stationed there; on guard; with guns in their holsters. It was an interesting sensation; and different, I realized, from that other time in the wintry darkness of the night, for then there had been people blindly under orders; now one had climbed; the air was different; the orders still came from somewhere else, but these people weren't passive, negative, confused: these were the people who knew what they were up to. And I felt (seeing those figures at the doors) how nice — how more than fortunate indeed! — that one had meant precisely what one had said. It must be a bit nasty to look back, in such a place, and feel one's conscience suddenly turn over!

Eventually we arrived somewhere, and I found myself seated in a normal-looking office, before a desk, as one might be anywhere. A middle-aged man was seated opposite: a man who goes by a short Russian name which my informed German friends were to tell me was a pseudonym. We were left alone. And the atmosphere which had been, downstairs in the lobby, about as cordial as a thicket of nettles, here was translated into something else. There was ease; urbanity; a glint of humor.

And just exactly what was it I had on my mind?

(Unpredictable little feminine mind! it was implied. But the note was delicate, even graceful — with only a soupçon of condescension; and the scrutiny that accompanied it was clinical enough.)

"Well — " I began. And found, sitting there in the heart of that building dedicated to the perverting and evading of truth, that the frank stating of one's own small tale suddenly was a matter of immense importance.

It was as if some crucial point were at stake. To speak the truth, that was the first part; to be believed — that was the second. For I found myself all at once wanting to be believed with a curious, a quite unprecedented intensity. Not for the sake of what I had come for. That was subsidiary; almost irrelevent. But as proof, I suppose — proof that the truth *could* be recognized. Anywhere; by anyone; even here.

I haven't put this very well; but it was one of those moments when one felt what all of us at times surely feel — a kind of passionate incredulity. How had this monstrous thing come to pass? This mythical splitting apart of humanity? Why were there such buildings? Such miasmic fears? One wanted to protest; to say something that would bring down the walls of Jericho.

Instead of which I said what I had come to say. "Well, it's simply this. I arrived in Berlin the night before last, and here's this Festival of yours, right here. And suddenly it seemed to me a bit stupid — it *would* be, wouldn't it? — not even to have a try at getting into it. For all I know, I'll never be on hand for such a thing again. So here I am. And you can ask me anything you want to ask, and look me over, and decide for yourself what my motives are."

And just what, he enquired pleasantly, did I wish to do?

"Well," I said, "I'd like to attend the opening ceremonies, of course. And be allowed to go anywhere, and talk with everyone, and to have it all — you know — clear and aboveboard. I mean, I don't want to be *suspected*, or any nonsense like that." And it occurred to me to add, "Last time when I tried to get to Berlin, I was held up — by your police. So I'd much prefer everything to be clearly understood, now, at the outset."

"And may I ask why? Why you wish all this?"

"Because I'm interested in learning what people are thinking. What it is they're afraid of, and what they hope for — how it all looks to them, from over here. You say this is a Festival in the cause of peace — "

"It is!" he said incisively.

"Then I'd like to see it. Very much indeed. Because I happen to care deeply about peace myself."

"And you'll write about it afterwards?"

"I expect so, eventually. I'm very slow," I explained. "Often it takes me ages to think things out."

"And you will write — sympathetically?"

I said, "Oh, come now!" We were both grown up!

There was a momentary glint. Almost of amusement.

"I'll write honestly," I stated. "The truth as I see it." And found myself adding, "You see, I believe something. I believe that the truth ultimately benefits everyone. That it serves us all."

I almost expected him to ask, like Pilate, "What is truth?" But he asked, instead, if I realized that there would be on hand, by tomorrow, a million or so people from all over the world, every one of them pining to get into a stadium that could accommodate the merest fraction of the number.

Certainly, I said. I quite realized it. That was why — to get in — I would have to have special credentials, wouldn't I?

It was at this point that he made a telephone call, turning aside and speaking rapidly and privately. Then he stood up. "Please — " he said. And away we again went, up another flight of stairs, and past more armed guards, and, at last, into an imposing room with a definite air to it, as if matters of some consequence were apt to occur here.

The sole occupant was a man in his early thirties; or so one judged: erect, straightforward-looking, extremely handsome, in a bright blue shirt with rolled-up sleeves. He might have graced an advertisement for United Steel, and was, as a matter of fact, the only man of this type I was to encounter at top level behind the scenes. I was introduced to him; we shook hands; then he and Mr. X stepped a little way off, speaking together in indecipherable tones. When they returned, we all sat down; and for what seemed to be an hour but was doubtless a quarter of it, questions were asked. And again one felt how unnerving it would be if it just so happened that one had something to hide! Every word, every nuance, every aspect of oneself was undergoing, obviously, the most severe of appraisals.

"But why," the younger man wanted to know, "just why did you decide to come here?"

"I suppose," I said, "because it seemed a good idea to start at the top."

And it was soon after this that I knew, inwardly, in that wordless way both familiar and inexplicable, that everything was going to be all right. And making the best of the sudden assurance, I said, "Of course, it would be awfully nice if I could have someone with me. An American friend. I mean, in all those millions of people it would help — wouldn't it? — to have an escort?"

For the first time, the only time, they both laughed. We all laughed together. An instant — that was all. Not complicated; not sardonic; not if it is truthfully to be recorded. (As a matter of fact, the request was to work: in due course credentials for Stephen were produced.)

The younger man now made a telephone call, his voice at first casual, then hardening with authority; and, after that, he wrote something down on a slip of paper. Alexanderplatz, Berolinahaus First Floor. I was, it appeared, to proceed to this address; I would be "expected."

We shook hands again. "Danke schön," I said. And meant it, too — for whatever it was that had tipped the scales, obviously I was the one who was profiting.

Then we walked downstairs again, Mr. X and I; and somehow or other we were speaking of poetry — because he asked me what kind of writing I liked best. *Poetry* we were talking about! of all things! There in the Informazionsministerium.

"All I know of yours is Pushkin," I said. "That one about 'The heavy-hanging chains will fall — ' "

"That is what must happen to all chains," he said.

"Then why are new ones so cruelly forged?"

"History," he said, "is a hard thing. It is made by those determined to make it. There is a process to be gone through. Only those who acknowledge it can expect to survive."

"I expect to survive," I allowed myself to say.

"And I," he said.

"But at my expense?"

"I would prefer it," he said, "at no one's expense. I'm afraid it will be for you to decide."

Afraid — afraid — the cancer at the heart.

Suddenly he took the slip of paper from my hand, and scribbled down something. "If it is necessary at any time to have — assistance," he said, "this number will reach me."

Downstairs, in the lobby, we formally shook hands.

I don't know who he was; I never saw him again.

The poem Pushkin wrote, a long time ago, he called "Message to Siberia."

> Deep in the Siberian mine,
> Keep your patience proud;
> The bitter toil shall not be lost,
> The rebel thought unbowed.
>
> The sister of misfortune, Hope,
> In the under-darkness dumb
> Speaks joyful courage to your heart:
> The day desired will come.
>
> And love and friendship pour to you
> Across the darkened doors,
> Even as round your galley-beds
> My free music pours.
>
> The heavy-hanging chains will fall,
> The walls will crumble at a word;
> And Freedom greet you in the light,
> And brothers give you back the sword.

This, then, was the Soviet Sector.

Seen at night, it had struck us as not only gloomy but sinister; now, in the brilliance of morning sun, as I made my way deeper and deeper into it — asking, "Bitte schön, Alexander-platz?" stared at by everyone, as if I'd dropped from the moon — now it had a look incommunicably drear. Dreariness beyond dreariness, in every direction, and imposed upon it, as by a massive hand, all the superficial paraphernalia of a state carnival. Flags flew everywhere; immense bright flags, splendidly streaming from tall masts, and thousands of little cotton ones, strung like bunting across the fronts of buildings pitted with shrapnel or still, at their tops, skeletonesque against the summer sky.

(Later one was to hear that it was expedient for all house-holders to fly flags; and it was also reported that the British and American ones were sold out first!)

Picasso's dove of peace began to crop up, on signs, in plaster — a stout matron of a bird: to incur, the following week in the *Berliner Zeitung*, official communist criticism for its lack of esprit! And now there were posters, of giant size and ranged in rows, and more of them and more as one proceeded inward: the orthodox Festival ones, all gaiety and garlands, and huge faces, cast in an implacable kindliness — Stalin, Grotewohl, President Pieck. Paul Robeson among them. And a woman, not known to me but, as a type, familiar enough, for it was the face of one who had achieved "equality" not by a sound expansion of identity but by de-womanizing herself into a quelling approximation of a man.

(In the days ahead this face was to be seen, in its incipient stages, time and again. On young women, on girls little more than children — matched to the kind of handclasps that hurt: to an ostentatious physical vigor, a ruthless repudiation of "femininity" that was to sharpen an earlier, half-developed impression. For I was to find myself remembering that day in San Francisco, when the Byelo-Russian delegation had turned up at the Conference, and I had raced to their headquarters in the basement of the Fairmont, having heard that they'd brought with them a woman delegate — a rumor of some interest, since Mr. Molotov's contingent had exhibited neither hide nor hair of such a creature. In a room, unpacking luggage, there they had been: a group of genial and strapping men. "Hello!" I had said to them. "Where is your woman?" "Woman?" they had repeated, as if a bit decadently one were implying something in black lace and a bed. We had heard, I'd explained, that there was one on the *delegation*. "Oh, no!" they had said. "Not a woman." "Well, you needn't sound so alarmed about it! Heaps of them are here. The British, you know, have brought two." And I had asked, because I was really interested, "Then *why* haven't you? Why haven't any Russian women been included? I thought you were so keen on that sort of thing." They had considered the point; then one of them had said, "It is very difficult, a very long journey, you understand." "What is?" I'd asked. "From Moscow," he had said. "From Moscow to here, it is very long. One must fly very high. The heart," he had said, and had fluttered his hand against a massive chest, "the heart goes so!" "You mean to tell me," I had asked, "that those women who drive tanks and helped defend Leningrad — " It was so manifestly preposterous that we had all laughed! Ruefully, good-humoredly, they had shaken their heads. When I'd spoken of it later in the day to Natalia she had said at once, "But there are many Russian women here; you are misinformed," and had pointed to the swarms of stenographers and secretaries. "Oh, Natalia," I'd said, "one doesn't mean *that!*" And hadn't meant, either, what the feminists mean! It was just that something had seemed, all at once, so inexorably male.)

Now, among the posters, there was suddenly a new note.

The "enemy" was appearing. And at the first view of Uncle Sam, malevolent as Boris Karloff, with, in one hand, an atom bomb, and blood dripping dramatically from the claws of the other, I stopped dead in my tracks. Then a goggled head, with a horrific explosion going on behind it, and the searing caption, to be everywhere encountered, "Truman Wants War!" Then the dove again; and the beautiful, fluent intermingling of flags; and "Freundschaft! Freundschaft! Freundschaft!" on all sides. On banners; on posters; as a word being spoken like a talisman on the air.

For "Freundschaft!" people were beginning to say, as, nearing Alexanderplatz, one found oneself moving through hordes of blue-shirted Freie Deutsche Jugend — Free German Youth. When I asked for directions, my hand was gripped. From now on in, at this level of contact, the keynote was to prove itself one of acceptance. I was a friend, obviously turned up from afar. Courageously I had managed somehow to arrive — for already the word was being hammered forth that the usual forces in the warmongering West had forcibly kept delegates from coming to Berlin.

"Thousands, thousands of Americans would be here," one was repeatedly to be told during the days following, "but your government was afraid to let them come!" And whose hands they played into — the visa difficulties raised by State Department and Foreign Office — is one of those points that plague our hour.

Now, at last, it was Alexanderplatz. And here, swarming the space so densely that one could only with difficulty inch a way through it, were the "Youth of the World": overwhelmingly, of course, in actual fact, the youth of East Germany.

Here were the young people being urged to "Fight for Peace." To "Demand the Abolition of the Atomic Bomb."

Here the generations being concentrated upon — shrewdly invested in — by the Politburo. (For increasingly, one was to hear from these young ones themselves, the older people in the Soviet Zone are being "written off.") Children, many of them, of ten and twelve; boys and girls in their teens; and young men and women through their middle twenties. Shabby, nondescript, muted-looking — in spite of the brilliance of their blue shirts. Buying, at stalls, little knitted caps banded with flags; buying small cakes of soap as if they were trinkets. A huge, slow-milling, inorganic mass. Not noisy, and not unmannerly either. Passive, pliable. That was how they struck one.

On the following day one was to see them otherwise. To see them, sure enough, like the youth on the posters: singing, striding, waving garlands of flowers. But here was only the raw material; or the instruments of the orchestra, with no baton yet raised. Just hordes and hordes of shabby young people, buying their little pieces of latherless soap; milling about aimlessly — some of them skeptical looking, even sardonic; many apathetic; but most, one felt, curious, uncertain, in a state of waiting.

"Freundschaft!" they said; not as one was later to hear the word — in a stupendous roar, in thundering waves of animal sound; but individually, almost experimentally, it seemed; and, when one smiled, they clasped one's hand.

Everywhere there were the signs "*Ami Go Home!*" But one's hand was clasped — because friendship, they supposed, had brought one here. A mother with a little boy, fair-haired and blue-eyed, not more than four, said to me, "Bitte schön," and to him, "Shake hands, Heini, with an American friend!" "American!" cried a group of older children, and all held up the little paper autograph books with which they seemed to have been supplied. Eagerly they showed off the names acquired. "From Hungary — from *China!* — " and one small girl said, "A black man in a skirt!" nearly bursting with the achievement of it.

Children. German children. Children who would ten years ago have been primed with the myth of a Master Race.

Something began to strike me. It was to strike harder every day.

Getting into the Berolinahaus was a bit of a feat, as hundreds of other people were trying to do the same thing; and finding Käthe like that, almost immediately, in the melee of journalists in a room marked *Presse*, was a happy stroke. She was behind one of the desks — some sort of junior official, I judged; and as soon as I spoke to her, mentioning from where I had just been sent, she said at once, "Oh, yes!" with a darting look of curiosity. She made a telehpone call; then, "Come, please," she requested, a quick change in her manner indicating that she was impressed. Apparently we were headed for another inner sanctum. And this one, I must say, nearly floored me.

For one found oneself, after a considerable wait, in a large room faced by, but some distance from, a man who seemed, both physically and mentally, the embodiment of what one had personally envisioned as "the real thing." There were other men present, four or five of them as I recall, standing about on the outskirts, so to speak: muscular, silent — reminding one of those mysterious, hefty individuals (with rosebuds in their buttonholes) who had circulated among the guests at a party of Mr. Molotov's. All that can be said about the likes of them is that they were disconcertingly *there*. It was the man opposite who had to be reckoned with.

Now conversations are something that, as a rule, I can remember with ease. Once the way they "felt" is inwardly revived, the words re-emerge, and even the exact tones in which they were spoken. But the twenty minutes or so that were spent in that particular room seem, when fixed upon, to resolve themselves not into a verbal exchange but into a peculiar intensity of awareness. I suppose because they were experienced in two sets of terms: as an outclash of words, going on hard and fast, but essentially as a realization at some under-level of thought.

The beginning I can recall, for he observed dryly, "And you say that you didn't, until you arrived, know that the Festival was taking place?"

"No, I knew nothing."

"How is that possible?"

"Easily so," I said. "I simply hadn't heard of it."

"Then you admit that the scurrilous Western press deliberately suppresses all such news?"

I almost said, "Why, you really say it, don't you!"

"It may have been bursting with the news," I told him. "I don't happen to have been seeing any papers lately."

"Yet you consider yourself an informed, reliable observer!"

"Just average," I said; and it occurred to me to note that if the scurrilous Western press suppressed all news, one would hardly — would one? — be any better off if one had been reading it. "If you really believed that, I should think you'd be pleased to have people turn up. To see for themselves."

"We're quite accustomed to having people turn up," he said, " — in the pay of their employers."

"Well, I'm not, alas, in anybody's pay." And I almost added that if I were, what a dandy mess of it I'd doubtless make!

He came in swiftly from another point. "And if you decided to tell the truth — you believe you'd be allowed to? It would be published, you think?"

I can't, myself, ever see that anything is gained in the world by a too facile claim.

"If it's true, yes, it's bound to be published. Sooner or later. I mean, the truth *comes out* — it always has, hasn't it? If not at once, and by way of oneself, then eventually, through someone."

"That," he said, "is reassuring indeed! If enough people in America are conceding *that* — "

One was, of course, no kind of match for him. For it was like having a conversation with a superbly disciplined and devious firefly. From one moment to the next one never knew where he would freakishly spark out; but all the time — how obvious! — he was precisely and split-secondly where he aimed to be. His attitude to begin with (if I gauged it correctly)was one of amused superiority; there was even an unconcealed edging of contempt. How on earth had this innocent ambled on to the scene! Something like that. His face was lean, ironic, acute. Everything about him gave one a feeling of controlled speed, of darting force; although throughout the interview he sat negligently in his chair, with scarcely a fingers' move discernible.

All one could do was to revert, stubbornly, to the main point: why one had come, what one wanted to do. And underneath the words there was that plunging realization, "This is it! Here it is!" The enemy-thing! And the realization, too, of how perilously we are apt to misappraise. For how we concentrate upon the *weight*, the *bulk*, the *power*, the iron rigidity of the basic doctrine — underestimating, as time and again we do, the enormous leeway of application; the lightning flexibility at certain levels; the authentic daring as unhitched to costs as it is to scruples.

For this man, it seemed to me, had a mentality as trained, as under control, as the athlete's body. And just as the athlete can convey an impression of weightlessness and ease, so here there was a sense of the utmost agility, of a capacity for sudden imaginative lunges that would knock the breath from the pedestrian plodder.

And I found myself thinking of those in the West, not converts but apologists, who still retain a kind of tag-end leniency: who discerned with passion and promptness and accuracy the evil of Fascism, but still balk at a final, unequivocal admission of what has come to pass under this other heading. (Often, it seems to me, because they dread — from a kind of muddled "sense of honor" — finding themselves classed with the professional penitents, with those who once having been totally taken in now make a career of crying "How I was fooled!") With what utter contempt, that was what struck one, such people must be regarded by a man like this! The contempt of the professional for the uninitiated amateur. It must be bottomless! That was what one felt.

And how fantastic to assume that anything less than the same caliber of conviction, the same skill and astuteness and scope of purpose, could be pitched against a phenomenon such as this.

Here he sat, this anonymous man: mercurial and yet immobile, making his thrusts from now one point, now another. And one would have given anything to understand the very heart of him, to be able to say, "What is it that drives you? Is it lust for power, as simple as that?" A contemporary ver-

sion of an immemorial urge. Or was there an outright madness of the mind: an unprecedented diabolism; a perversion —
so deliberate, absolute, and precise — of the moral order, that
the true and the false, from where he operated, were literally
interchangeable.

Whatever it was, one thing at any rate stood plain enough.
At the final count, the challenge must be met, and the war
won, on the level of ideas. For how could a mental force like
this be bombed from the world? Smash it in one place, it
would leap from another. For it was something that has
happened in human consciousness, and however imperative
the physical action, the surgical operations that society must
resort to, in the end that infinitely more difficult thing must
be somehow done. The enemy must be mentally outmatched;
outendured. *From the standpoint of vision, he must be out-
thought.*

Again, at a certain moment and for no reason that I can
name, there was the feeling that it was going to be all right.
Permission would be granted; I felt suddenly relaxed; and it
was soon after this that we both stood up, and the man walked
with me across the room and opened the door.

"I should be interested," he said, "in talking with you
further. When you've watched it all, come back and see me."

But I wasn't to go back; I never saw him again.

Outside the door, Käthe took me in hand — assigned, one
gathered, to supervise whatever remained to be done. "Who
was he?" I asked her, as we walked away; and she said, "The
Direktor!" adding, in the tone of a very minor official, "It is
the first time I have ever seen him!"

We were in another room now with a group of students.
Art students from Leipzig, they turned out to be, who were

receiving, with their instructions, some sort of special card of admission, because tomorrow, at the stadium, they were to make drawings and take photographs of the opening ceremonies. "For the official record!" they eagerly explained — all tremendously exhilarated in their blue shirts and little caps: importantly "included" in monumental doings!

The artist, suddenly one became aware. The one so apt in our own society to be the disparaged, the discounted member; or indulgently relegated to the status of a divertissement; or, if sufficiently endowed and celebrated, exempt from adult responsibility (genius suspended luminously in a vacuum, because conceived of as some sort of sub-citizen) — here feeling himself an integral part of something, not a clique, but the world-at-large of his fellows: acknowledged, accepted, of specific use, and, if privileged, only in proportion to his certifiable value. For that, it seemed to me, was how it must feel. If one were a student, and very young; knowing war and defeat and utter disintegration. And with nothing in between, no interval of light — for how that fact must be taken into account, in all our policy calculations! This particular generation, these younger Germans, what had they to turn to as a touchstone in their past? Their parents knew a different order of things. But they themselves, hurled from Hitlerism into a Stalinist world, what had they to compare but one falsity with another? (It was Ernst who was to say, "Under Hitler we were taught that only Germans matter; now we've learned that the people is a great brotherhood.") They had known disaster and chaos and loss. And because they were young and had, too, however slight their talent or miserably misdirected, this instinct to create, this point of sensibility from which have flowered all the grace-things of life — how vulnerable they were! how in need of reassurance! how exhilarated by the "proof" here afforded them that they and their gifts were valued in the world.

At the spectacle of the artist, self-betrayed, one stands aghast. Violating, as it does, verities at the very heart of our civilization. It can even, I suppose, in some intimate way seem a more shocking, a more traitorous thing — the coming to terms with a slave state of the painter, the poet, the novelist, the musician — than the crimes committed on a political level. And yet isn't there something to be understood, too? If one is accurately to deal with this hour?

"Freedom," we say, "to create as I choose." But freedom, a fine place, can be also a lonely one. In freedom can be found, as well as the fulfilled, the frustrated, the neglected, the embittered, the adrift. The artist, too callously cast into freedom, may, instead of flowering, negatively shrivel up — curiously unnourished by a plenitude of disregard! "Freedom!" we say; insisting upon the word; coming dangerously close, it would sometimes seem, to making a fetish of one half of a truth, in a world where the bereft, the disenfranchised, the lost, are seeking, perhaps, more deeply than freedom, the assurance of kinship; of a common hearth; of being in some way fitly joined together.

If we miss the loneliness at the heart of men, how we miss the point at which they are won.

Kurt, very tall, with his Leica handsomely strapped to a shoulder, and wearing with a kind of studio casualness the inevitable blue shirt, said, "It is a wonderful thing, yes? So many people! Hundreds of Americans will be here tomorrow!" (Behindhand, it would seem: still stuck with a previous line of information.) "You will be at the stadium?" he wanted to know.

"Yes, I think so."

"Good, then I will look for you; perhaps we will meet."

(As a matter of fact, astoundingly we were to do so.)

And there was a girl called Liesl behind a desk, who said, as she filled out some sort of form, "You will find many church groups with us here, and that is what I am so happy about! Because it's we, of the churches, who can do the most — for friendship and peace." Liesl of whom I was to see something more: sunny-faced, warm, so glad I was here. (Had she an equally sunny-faced mother who, ten years before, had been ardently saying, "Our dear Führer! how he toils for us all"?)

The boys with their cameras; the girl with her churches.

Nobody, it would seem, was being left out!

We were all in a group, talking together; and one of them said, "But you don't sound like an American — not like the G.I.'s I heard once." So I explained that I had spent my life between countries, and had in consequence a mongrel sort of speech; and Käthe at once said to me, with something new in her voice, "I lived in England, for seven years."

"You did?" I was surprised; for she couldn't be out of her twenties yet, so that seven years was a sizable piece of life.

"I went there in 1938," she said. "My father and mother were killed by the Nazis, and I was taken away. Both my children were born in London." And she said, "The English are a fine people — I saw them through the war, how they behaved. They are very brave, and very kind. And they don't feel sorry for themselves, the way the Germans do."

Only afterwards did I realize how she had phrased that. When people in Germany speak about themselves they say, almost invariably, I've found, "we Germans," "us Germans" — as if, by insisting upon it, they could bring into being that longed-for unity which they, of all mature peoples in the world, have never had. And therefore seek, as philosophers and poets, or fanatically lay claim to, under daemonic leadership, with the urgency of those feeling themselves somehow "left out" of an historic process shared by the rest of us. ("So that we have no focal point, nothing to rally around," Friedl had once said to me, pointing out how she, in her own lifetime, had seen three different flags fly over her country: the Schwarz-Weiss-Rot, the Kaiser's Reich; the Schwarz-Rot-Gold, the Weimarer Republik; then Hitler's Swastika, the Hakenkreuzfahne; and the Schwarz-Rot-Gold again. "In Germany we have no national holiday, no July the Fourth, or Bastille Day; we've no Magna Carta, or Marseillaise, or Abraham Lincoln, or impersonal Crown. We haven't even a song — with all our songs — that stands for us all. We are without a symbol.")

Käthe, I was to realize, had said "the Germans." As if she were speaking from another category: out beyond nation, out beyond race.

It was late in the evening when the line was again crossed; and when, at last, I made my way back to Regina's flat it was to find everybody there in a state of what appeared to be genuine alarm. Several telephone calls were at once made — "She's back! she's safe!" "But of course I am!" I said, tired enough to feel that anything could be breezed into: the Kremlin itself. "We have lived here," said Regina, "a long, long time. There is no 'of course' in this sort of world."

I showed them my booty, an official pass, and a ticket marked N *Sitzplatz Block H*; and they wrote down and later reported to someone else (a friend "working with" the Americans at a consequential level) the telephone number given me in the Informazionsministerium. Then we all went to bed. Tomorrow loomed. The grand opening of the *Welt-*

jugendfestspiel: which I was, it so happened, to witness for three of those seven or eight hours — quite inadvertently, without knowing where I was — from the Russian press box in the company of Ernst.

III

"Is it not beautiful! Is it not good! Here is the whole world come together!"

I looked up at him, Pauli, the boy standing there beside me in the bright blue shirt of the Freie Deutsche Jugend; and his face was radiant; there was no other word for it.

"Now you can tell them how it is," he said, "that here there is freedom — that all may come!"

And Ernst, older, in his late twenties, I judged, wearing the dark uniform of the Volkspolizei (but without any insignia, so that it wasn't until the following day that I learned his rank), said with pride, "It has been heavy for us here in Berlin, but — *it is done!*" And he was saying then, suddenly, as he pointed up, "Look! can you see?" For in a momentary lull another sound could be heard, a minute buzz, as if a pin were drilling; and there, just discernible in the profundities of blue, was a helicopter. It was circling about, inquisitive but prudently keeping at a fixed distance.

"From the West!" Ernst said. "Like an angry bee!"

And they all laughed. So easily, and with such confidence, he and the several other young men who had gathered around sociably, eager to talk, that their assumption was more than ever apparent. Because I was here, really seeing it, I must inevitably perceive the "truth" of what was going on.

It was a superb vantage point, this concrete box — high above the whole Walter Ulbricht stadium and immediately overlooking the main entrance. Below us, massed together, were some seventy thousand spectators: tier upon tier of them in the blaze of summer sun, with their tanned arms lifted high above their heads as the rhythmic clapping now deepened, now lightened, and the cry of "Freundschaft! Freundschaft!" surged up — subsiding at one point, breaking out at another, but in a marking-time sort of way, one felt, coming as yet only from throats, not sounding as soon it would begin to sound as if drawn from the very guts of these boys and girls. In the center of the stadium there was a great square of grass, theatrically vacant, with geometric designs scribbled on it in colored chalks ("Like a Picasso," I said to Ernst; but Picasso, it appeared, had better stick to his doves!) and bordered by the smooth tan of a roadway wide enough to take abreast twenty marchers. There were several encampments of photographers, one saw — had Kurt managed to find his Leipzig group? — and quantities of police, all over the place, accenting darkly the blocs of gala yellows and blues, the crimson and white of delegation costumes; and there were Russian soldiers planted about, less numerous, more static, in stocky little clumps: looking, as they were to look wherever encountered, isolated, islanded, unsure of themselves — *glum* was the word that each time came to me: like children obliged by a powerful parent to remain at a party to which they hadn't been invited. Up here, at our own level, flags flew splendidly from immense white staffs, the flags of all nations, in an unbroken circle; and raised up between them, in great bold letters, was the appropriated word: the word blazoned, chanted, dinned from loudspeakers. "Peace — Paix — Friede

— Paz — Pace — Pax — NMP — " And there was something else, too, to be seen from this height: beyond the rim of the stadium an upjutting of shapes, fixed, friezelike, against the brilliant sky. The ruins of Berlin. So bleached, so stripped and abstracted from here that they might have been the bones of some antique city. A ghostly presence at the edge of the feast. The shouting and the singing boys and girls — and the empty sockets, the derelict joints.

Now the music had suddenly come to a pause. There was a taut silence; and now, from trumpets, the kind of fanfare that anywhere at all can send down the spine a shock of excitement. A great roar broke into the air; in an instant the whole stadium had massively risen. It was starting! They were coming! Here they were! — the spectacularly diversified special delegates, nearly twenty thousand of them, from sixty-six countries. "All the world!" Undeniably so! As swinging through the entrance, erect, heads high, with their flags and garlands and pageantlike regalia, out they came into the sunlit space: inexhaustibly, it was to seem, for hour after tumultuously occupied hour; each group marching the full round of the stadium and then assuming a position on the great central square.

Albania, Algeria, Austria, Afghanistan — Australia and Brazil, Belgium, Burma — nation after nation and race upon race, with their arms flung up in comradely salute as again and again the greeting thundered out. *"Freundschaft! Freundschaft! Freundschaft!"* from the crowd, and the word called back again by the marching lines, the Mexicans in sombreros, the Frenchmen in berets, the South Africans and West Indians and Turks and Swedes; the Czechs, waving olive branches, and the Poles, bearing high on slender staffs a shining-silver sea of papier mâché doves; Spaniards, Saudi Arabians, Pakistani, Lebanese; Greeks and Indonesians and Italians and Finns; Iraqi and Peruvians, Egyptians and Dutch, and, from Mongolia, tall regal black men in emperorlike robes, pacing ceremoniously to a sudden acceleration of roars from the crowd, as if the more "different" and from "far away," the more wonderful the friends, the more meaningful their being here.

The large German contingent from the Western Zones ("See, they are with us!" Pauli cried) and the Germans from the East: here they were, too. The young people one had yesterday seen milling about, buying pieces of soap in Alexanderplatz: shabby, nondescript, signifying nothing. From their factories and farms and offices and schools, from wherever it was they had been summoned and brought, here they were: proudly, vigorously bearing themselves — young people granted the entrance of heroes. Shapers of the future! striding out, like this, into a blinding blaze of "universal" fellowship. . . .

Ernst touched his bottle of Apfelsaft to mine. "To friendship — to the friendship of all the people!" he said. And Pauli said radiantly, joining in, "To our beautiful Festival!"

We stood there high above the whole brilliant scene. It was the finest possible place from which to watch. But it wasn't, of course, N *Sitzplatz Block H.*

In the morning, at the point in the British Sector which Regina had decided would be nearest the stadium, after showing my pass to the Eastern police — solidly massed across the street — I'd been allowed through the barricade and had turned, for a moment, to wave Auf Wiedersehen to the friends who had escorted me thus far. "Do be *careful!*" they had enjoined, standing there in the West a few feet away. But in a

matter of minutes there'd been no care to take; there'd been
nothing to decide — one went, that was all; borne like a
cork on a great flood of blue shirts.

It was, I suppose, the biggest crowd I've ever been involved
in myself. A sea of people, in every direction, all converging
upon a center, with cordons of Volkspolizei repeatedly slowing us and the sound of bands flaring from now this point,
now that, as last minute delegations came, very fast, through
a cleared passageway. ("Rumania!" people noted: line upon
line of girls in middy blouses. "Chile — Denmark — ") The
walls of the stadium loomed ahead. But some distance from
it we found ourselves brought to a sudden standstill, with the
word passed back to us from those in front that the gates had
been closed; no more were being admitted. Whether everybody had a ticket, I don't know; but there we all stood —
balked but unbudged; and since I couldn't think of anything
else to do I held up my pass, at arm's length, and called into
the air, "Press! Press!" It sounded about as effectual as a
bird-pipe at Niagara. But suddenly, calling back, there was
Kurt.

He was towering above the immediate seethe of shirts, looking battered, harrassed, and clutching his camera like the Holy
Grail; and the sight of him was so heartening that I could
have wept. "Oh, Kurt!" I cried, "whatever shall we do?"
As if we'd been intimates for years and years. He had shoved
a way over; he was confirming the report. Yes, it was so: the
doors of the stadium had been closed some time ago; he'd
been clean around to each of the entrances and this, if we
could possibly manage to get to it, was the one for us to
reach with our special passes. "Come on then," I said (we
were speaking English), "let's both of us yell!" And "Press!
Press!" he shouted too, until people around us began to offer

advice — which was nice of them, only afterwards I was properly to realize, since they all must have wanted to get in as much as we did. "You must find," said someone, "an officer of the Russian Army." The point, one inferred, of final authority. And someone else suddenly was gesturing to the left. "Look, over there!" An officer of the Russian Army, sure enough — three of them, in fact: standing solid, gray, and set off by a little margin of empty space. But Kurt (for whatever his reasons were) seemed sharply disinclined to initiate a contact; he even shook his head at me, and shoved us both deliberately in the opposite direction. And it was at this point, as we were floundering, and pretty well stumped, that Ernst appeared.

If he had been "planted" there — as certain friends afterwards were immediately to conclude — then it was a miracle of management, that's all one can say; and an astounding amount of strategy for so picayune a case. Shouldering a way over to us from wherever he had been, he asked, in English, "What's the trouble? Can I help you?" He spoke with a strong Midwest accent (which was because of someone called Hank, in Nebraska); he was tall, well set, and with, I was to learn, two different faces, an open one and a closed. At the moment he looked like any young man offering to be of service.

When we showed him our passes, he said at once, "Follow me." And whether he spoke a word, or presented inconspicuously some sort of credential, I have no idea; but the crowd promptly parted for him, person by person, with Kurt and myself plunging along at his heels. It was a knockabout business, until Ernst, suddenly turning and looking down, said, "Your feet!" (I was wearing sandals composed only of a strap or two, not much protection in this jungle of boots.) And after that he walked backwards, providing a small space for me to step in safely until we reached the entrance, where, within moments, a door was unbolted by one of the guards; and there we all were, the three of us, inside.

Kurt was given directions for reaching his group. "Auf Wiedersehen, Fräulein!" "Auf Wiedersehen, Kurt!" He hared off; it was the last I was to see of him. Then I presented my own Block ticket; but Ernst, after a glance, returned it to me. "I'll take you to a better place than that," he said; and up we started, rapidly climbing from level to level and, as we climbed, talking together. At some point or other names were exchanged (I being one of those who can't rest easy until this is done); and somewhere else we paused, while he pointed out certain of the stadium arrangements.

"It is very good — you will see! It takes much work to make a beautiful thing."

He spoke in such a way that I turned, interested. "You sound as if you'd designed it yourself!"

"That is what I should like to do."

"Festivals? I said. "Design festivals?"

"No, design for the stage — for our Berlin theater."

How boundlessly unpredictable, even Volkspolizei!

"Then why not, why don't you?" I wanted to know.

He merely said, "Later. When it is possible."

I assumed that he meant he wasn't allowed to, and must, I suppose, have implied as much; for he at once stated, "You misunderstand." And it was then that he said something still fixed in my head. "For me there exist three things. First, world peace. Second, a united Germany. Third, myself." He spoke with an austerity not often heard, not when men speak of what they personally wish to do; and I was to be given no reason, in the days that followed, to doubt that the words were formidably meant.

When at last we reached it, the box at the top, I said, "Oh, Ernst, what a place to see from!" There were chairs there, ranged before a shelf to write on, and telephones, and bottles of Apfelsaft produced, and even sharpened pencils when I couldn't find my own; there were Pauli, and the several other Freie Deutsche Jugend — all of us in a corner, in a group by ourselves, with so much going on and to be taken in that, at this stage, the rest of the occupants were barely noticed. I did, to be sure, register a little galaxy of Russian officers, and police coming and going, and a squad of camera men; and some twenty or so other people, including three or four women, who presumably were "the press" since they weren't in uniform. But that, I'm afraid, was literally all. And that was how I happened to be where I was.

Now three hours later, and in the middle of the afternoon, the last of the delegations had swung around the course. The Chinese had come — rank upon rank of scarlet silk flags, borne high in the air by ebony-headed boys in slate-gray suits and followed by girls with garlands of white flowers which they waved lyrically like a movement in a dance. The British had come, a small contingent, outlandishly including a lone Scotsman in kilts: all ambling on to the scene (it couldn't possibly be called marching) — the young women in rather rumpled, un-doctrinaire voiles, with droopy cardigans, and strings of beads, and their stocking seams crooked, one didn't doubt; the men, in gray flannels, with tweed jackets or striped blazers. *English!* one would instantly and anywhere have known, without a sign or a syllable to announce their origin. Incorrigibly English, and therefore, the lot of them, looking so ludicrously out of key with the occasion (just as they were casually out of step with one another) that the greeting accorded them seemed to falter a trifle — it being, one supposed, a bit difficult to maintain a grandiose roar with people who waved back, pleasantly and nonchalantly, as if to an aunt on a Brighton platform. . . . The United States delegation had traipsed around. Nine nondescript persons trying hard to look more, with the only bold thing about them a placard that stated "American Youth Joins Hands With The Youth Of The World!"

Pauli had exclaimed, "And now — America!" (The Turks had just passed.) But when the showing turned out to be so measly a one, I could feel him, like a host with an embarrassed guest, undertaking to mitigate the chagrin assigned to me!

"We know how many *would* have come," he said. "We know they are our friends — the American youth."

"Why do you think many of them would have come?" I asked.

And he said, "Because the youth — they don't want war. They would work with us for peace, if they were allowed to understand."

How many true things were to be said, alas! The wrong way round.

When the North Koreans strode into the sun, the whole stadium had risen instantly in one great surge. They had marched out proudly, but without aplomb: vigorous, confident — straight from action, it was easy to believe — with the several women in the first two rows handsome, gallant-looking, their battledress glinting with decorations, all that the eye could ask as "heroines." Wave upon thundering wave of welcome had broken upon them. "Paix — Pace — Friede

— Paz — " The word blazoned high between the flying flags, and there, down below, the khaki figures, the "fighters for peace". . . . At the end had marched the Union of Soviet Republics. Hundreds strong, and dressed all in white, they had swung through the entrance with their tanned arms lifted high above their heads; and instantly, as their hands had come together, in an electrifying clap, tens of thousands of arms had gone up throughout the stadium. The handbeat had steadied into a mesmeric rhythm: the giant pulse of a single organism. And *"Freundschaft! Freundschaft! Freundschaft!"* it had come — the roar now brought to an animal-like intensity as the long ranks marched with lifted heads, with an effect of inexhaustible, irresistible vitality; like athletes and dancers, like participants in a rite. The Russian soldiers left out, isolated in groups — but these boys and girls under the selfsame orders, from the selfsame place, hailed, clasped. At what level of camaraderie? how crucially to be reckoned with in the world we share?

Now, at last, in the middle of the afternoon, all were assembled. Sixty-six blocs, a bright forest of flags: "the whole world" finally here before us. The music had stopped short. There was a dramatic stillness. "Watch!" Ernst said to me, speaking quietly. And suddenly something happened that was extraordinarily beautiful.

Suddenly from below, from the center of the stadium, twenty thousand pigeons were loosed into the air. Upward they broke with a great whir of wings: first in a lovely chaos of movement, then all swiftly slanting clean into the sun, and a moment or two afterwards as swiftly turning — level upon level of them: now white, now glittering as if fashioned from silver — to slant all together another way. For a trancelike instant their wings were held still. A cloud-drift of birds, silent, sunstruck. And from the stadium rose a curiously moving sound. Softly, wonderingly, childlike it came, a great low "Ah — " into the quietened air. Thousands upon thousands of upturned heads, of young faces lifted to the mounting birds.

"Ah, schön! — schön — " Pauli exclaimed.

I turned to look at him, and he might have been a child, simplified to so pure and candid a delight. And it was then that I found out where I was.

For beyond his lifted and lighted face I saw, suddenly, the faces of the others. Speculative, hardened, clinical, sardonic. The faces of the people casually sitting there, watching, not the birds, but the effect upon a mass of a skillful trick.

It was a queer feeling. Like an elevator drop.

"Ernst," I said, "where are the rest of them?"

"The rest?" he asked.

"The Americans, the British — the rest of the press?"

"Oh, the Western press isn't here," he said; and added, matter-of-factly, "It's over there."

What he pointed to was the other side of the stadium, which appeared, suddenly, some miles off.

Carefully I glanced around the box; and for the first time realized that my presence had hardly gone unnoticed. Army officers; Volkspolizei; Russians and Poles and Bulgarians and Czechs —

Ernst asked, "What's the matter?"

"I don't think I ought to be here, Ernst! This isn't my place!"

He glanced around, too. He looked competent, sure of himself. After a moment he said (and I never did remember to ask him why), "You would like me to take you over to your friends?"

We had spoken between ourselves; and when I turned, with an involuntary sense of urgency, Pauli and the others appeared flabbergasted; then dismayed. "But you aren't *leaving!*" Why it had only started! There were hours more to come! (As indeed there were.)

"No, no, I'm not leaving. I'm just going — somewhere else." And I assured them, "I'll stay till the end, I promise you!"

Pauli said earnestly, "It *is* beautiful, isn't it? You can see how beautiful!" For I was to carry the news of it to those who hadn't come: I was to bear back the truth to the benighted West.

We said Auf Wiedersehen, shaking hands; and I felt as if I were leaving on a sinking raft a boy it would be no pleasure to see drown.

It took us a long while to circle the stadium; and, as we went, speeches were being militantly hurled into the air. "Today Berlin is a city of youth — " "Which side are you on, young people of the world — " "Long live the free German youth! Long live the co-operation of youth the world over — " The more sweeping, the more embracing the phrases rung out, the wilder, one realized, the response evoked; and when I spoke of this to Ernst, he said, "Yes, it is," and he said then what I already have written down. "Under Hitler we were taught that only Germans matter; now we've learned that the people is a great brotherhood."

We came out eventually at the opposite side of the stadium. We were among packed benches — Block H it was — with people squashed together in considerable discomfort, and all mixed up, so far as one could determine, for Ernst tapped on the shoulder somebody who must have been a German, for he at once obediently vacated his place. There was a quick bit of shuffling; then I found myself inserted between a London journalist and the Berlin correspondent of one of the great New York dailies — a man of whom Regina and her professional friends had spoken with both respect and gratitude, saying, "He really cares what happens!" — that tribute which seems sometimes the highest that can be paid. And I felt, suddenly, something that I was startled to find myself experiencing. An almost physical sensation of kinship. One's own kind again! Faces one could trust! Concepts rooted deep in the mind and heart. If one were to say "the Mad Hatter's Tea party — " or "of the people, by the people — " or "the quality of mercy is not strained — " they would know what one meant: we shared touchstone upon touchstone, assumption after assumption. However sharp or numerous our disagreements might be, we belonged, with ease and certainty and warmth, to the same moral order.

I was startled, almost shocked. Believing, as I do, in a raceless and placeless country of the mind attainable by all who transcend frontiers. And at the same time realizing, "This is what Pauli and the rest of them have never had. This is what they grasp for — to be at ease, to belong."

One must, I suppose (rudely planted there), have been something of a surprise.

"Hullo!" somebody said, "where have you come from?"

"Well, as a matter of fact — " But I found that I didn't quite know how to phrase it! Just as there was some difficulty in explaining Ernst. Presumably he had ousted another German, for there he now was, seated behind me, with a guardian-like, almost a proprietory air. "You are comfortable, yes?" "Oh, yes, this is fine." He leaned forward, with authority pointing things out. (The dense square of delegations was flooding fluently apart: the whole dispersal accomplished with spectacular speed.) He spoke exclusively to me, as if the others didn't exist; and when the Englishman, in an undertone, asked, "Who is he?" I felt a bit stumped. "Well — he's Ernst. He's rather — you know — taken me under his wing." "Evidently!" he said, his voice dry. And when the American, half turning, casually over his shoulder asked a question — something about the disposition of the groups: for the gymnastic displays were now beginning, on a scale and with a brilliance of execution that I had never, myself, seen the like of before — Ernst answered him so curtly, in so inflexible a fashion, that I glanced around: seeing a face closed, impassive, giving nothing; a quite different face; as if he were conducting himself in enemy territory.

The afternoon massively rolled on and on. There would never, it seemed, be an end to the thing, to the energy, the ingenuity, the outpouring multiplicity of performers. There was something frighteningly inexhaustible to it all: as if the voices would never tire, the beating hands fail; as if behind this, the immediate spectacle, and behind all these, the visible participants, stretched dim and monstrous reserves of strength. A shadowy world of restless men. Groping, semi-emerged: the dead past done with for better or for worse. . . .

Hour upon tumultuously occupied hour. And then, again, suddenly a moment loosed into beauty — meaning more than the birds; more sobering than that; because involving a verity at the very heart of our hour. From somewhere a sound of singing began. It seemed to start spontaneously, at the other end of the stadium, and gradually, lightly, to widen out until the whole huge throng, moved to its feet, was standing with lifted arms intimately linked, swaying, like fields all touched by the same wind — swaying, singing, with the sound rising soft and deep into the air (an old Russian folk tune, later one was to learn) gentle and melodious, as if children sang.

I turned towards Ernst; and he said, "It is the Song of the Youth of the World. All are singing it in their own languages."

Tens of thousands of boys and girls. From the north, from the south, from the islands of the sea; yellow and white and black of skin; from seashore and mountain, steppes and veldt.

"Jugend aller Nationen, uns vereint gleicher Sinn, gleicher Mut!" sang the young Germans.

> Wo auch immer wir wohnen, unser Glück auf dem Frieden
>   beruht.
> In den dusteren Jahren haben wir es erfahren:
> Arm ward das Leben! Wir aber geben Hoffnung der müden
>   Welt!
> Unser Lied die Ländergränzen überfliegt, Freundschaft siegt!
>   Freundschaft siegt!
> Ueber Klüfte, die des Krieges Hader schuf, springt der Ruf,
>   springt der Ruf:
> Freund, reih' dich ein, dass vom Grauen wir dieWelt befrei'n!
> Unser Lied die Ozeane überfliegt, Freundschaft siegt!
>   Freundschaft siegt!

The sound of it was a beautiful sound on the air. Not militant, not vehement, but gentle as if the voices were reaching out not only to one another but to regions beyond and beyond all this. There were tears on some of the faces one could see — the faces of young singers standing with linked arms. And suddenly I was blinded by tears myself. For however falsely, however treacherously and cruelly it was being used, this impulse of the heart, this longing, this outwardness — here it was in the world, both flower and force. And perhaps it was fitting that the tears should come. Perhaps, confronted by this choir-like sound, it was well for a moment to leave confidence and pride, and ask, in humility, "*Wherein have we failed?*"

> Unser Herzen erglühn, und den Schwur wiederhold jeder
> Mund:
> Restlos Wolln wir uns mühen, dass kein Feind mehr zerschlägt
> unsern Bund.
> Bruderliche Gedanken überwinden die Schranken.
> Reicht euch die Hände, nun sich vollende
> Glück der Gemeinsamkeit!
> Unser Lied —

"Freundschaft siegt!" I wanted to sing too — rescuing the words, saving them for a truer world.

Now the sun had dropped behind the rim of the stadium, and below us, in a kind of golden dusk, there was a soccer game going on between an East German team and one from Russia. ("Is it possible," I asked the American correspondent, "for the Germans to win?" and he said merely, "What do you think!") I can't remember exactly when the shirt was spoken of; but at some point I happened casually to remark, "Can anybody, I wonder, buy a blue shirt?" and at once Ernst said, "You would like to have one?" I decided that I would — to take back to America. "Tomorrow then," he said. "If you will come again."

Afterwards I was to ask him why he had done this.

"Why did you treat me differently, Ernst?"

"Because," he was to say, "you are different."

"But different from what, different from whom? I, too, belong to the West."

"I watched them, those others — those newspaper men."

And he was to say, harshly, "They looked at us with hate!"

"Oh, *no*, Ernst! It's not true! Not with *hate!*"

"I saw how they looked."

"But not hatred of people! Of something else. They care about people as much as you do — certainly as much as I do, I can assure you of that. I know such men; I know what they think."

But his face was to remain inexorably set.

Now, in the stadium, I said, "Of course I'll come again! When — where?"

Herr Eisler's Ministerium seemed pitched a bit high; so the Berolinahaus was decided upon, the only other building I knew how to head for. At three o'clock, Ernst specified, in the Presse department; and it was soon after this that he stood up suddenly and announced that he must leave; he was due back on duty.

"You will find your way home?"

"Oh, yes, don't worry; I'll be all right."

"Wear more shoes on your feet," he advised; and he said, too, "Tomorrow I will show you *our* Berlin."

I thanked him for his courtesy, and he was quickly gone. Chief, I was to learn, of the border police.

IV

The next morning, with the doors opened wide on to the balcony and the linden trees gala with summer light, we sat for ages around the breakfast table, endlessly drinking cups of Nescafé. Regina and Tante and the Herr Professor from Dresden, and Klaus, of course, and Gerhardt who was another ex-Wehrmacht officer, and Stephen, and a German neighbor or two — all wanting to hear about everything that had occurred.

In the room were the things salvaged from a home destroyed. Regina's piano and the small Dürer, the fine books that were apt, when one picked them from shelves, to be scorched at an edge or pitted with shrapnel: remnant of the library that had belonged once to the father who had been one of Germany's great scholars. A gemütlich room, in which one found oneself intimately at home. So that if it had suddenly been decreed "Here you must remain for the next twelve months" one would have said "Oh, good!" — already established; with this gaiety to draw upon, this courage and warmth; these values that seemed more congenially defined than many a pattern in one's own society. For when people have known peril and horror and loss, and have survived not only with integrity intact but with a health, a humor, rooted in some morally achieved sense of proportion, there comes into their attitude a kind of ease, almost a carelessness towards much that once mattered. Nothing has been rejected; it isn't that. It's simply, one feels, that the props are now negligible, so that all the symbols of "status" and "security" — the formalities and proprieties so essential to those unsure of themselves — are held casually or as casually done without: like Meissen china used in a kitchen or, in a drawing room, Woolworth crockery.

(It was Madeleine who had said once, "How *serious* they are!" — we had bolted from the same excruciatingly genteel dinner party. "When you eat in a ditch, from a sack," she had said, "you wipe the grease from your mouth with the back of your hand." "But that — good heavens! — is because it's *eating!* An animal act! Don't you like things sublimated!

Didn't you fight for the refinements of life!" "For Bach," she had said, "for certain poetry, perhaps, and the civilities between people as well as the principles. But not, I think, for a finger bowl!" Madeleine with her fastidious ear and eye, and palate too, discriminating expertly at a concert, a gallery, a lecture, a ballet, between the first rate and the second. Madeleine who at twenty had joined the Resistance; gnawed turnips; slept on mountainsides; survived all Ravensbrück.)

A certain ease one can find, almost a carelessness — when people know within themselves, as a proven fact, how stripped a man can stand, and nevertheless *be*.

We sat there talking around the ample breakfast table; and everybody, as I told them about the stadium ceremonies, kept saying, "Ah, yes — " The tale almost wearisomely familiar, I suppose.

"Ah, yes," said Regina, "and the pigeons too!"

"They were *beautiful*, Regina — extraordinarily so!"

"But of course," she said, "they always are. Pigeons can be relied upon, every time."

And the Herr Professor said, "Now you can see how it was, when Hitler did it. There is no difference; it is precisely the same."

But this was something I couldn't agree with; I never can. "But I don't think it is — not precisely the same. All the trickery may be, but surely the myths are two different myths. How could there have been that song, for instance; or anything like it?"

"Oh, songs! Liebling. People sang their heads off!"

"But not a song like that! You couldn't have had it! A Nazi rally was addressed to *Germans*, wasn't it? — to the 'volk,' the 'blood,' to that fancy 'race soul'? What could it have said to a Mongolian, or a Korean? Yesterday it was different, because there they all were — all of them together, black and white and yellow and brown. Nazism might have conquered the world, but it could never have *seduced* it. Not like this. It was your own personal sickness; a group malady."

"Evil is evil," the professor said. "The same root, the same flower."

Which was true, of course. And on one level, certainly, they must be equated, the Horst Wessel song and the song of World Youth: an administered mass mesmerism, to right or to left. But the distinction, it seemed to me, crucially remained.

And Klaus, the cousin (with those five years behind him of imprisonment in Russia), said to the uncle, "Evil may be evil, yes, it is so; but each phase of it must be accurately diagnosed by us. A man with a cancer and a man with small-pox, they are both sick men. But the physician will prescribe for them different treatments. If he wishes to cure, he will be precise." And he said, then, "It is a dangerous thing, about us Germans, that we can, in one area, be the most scrupulously exact of peoples, but in another we seem deliberately to blur all lines. If the statement is made to us 'Fascism is a cancer and Communism a small pox' — what do we do? We are wounded; we wince away; we shrink from a comparison. Because at once we assume that we're being told 'Smallpox isn't as bad as cancer!' We see, in every attempt to diagnose, only a further indictment of Germans — an attempt to excuse others at our expense."

"When really," I said, "it hasn't anything to do with *better* or *worse*. That isn't what one means at all!"

"It's the nature of the thing," Klaus declared. "It's what part of a man is made use of by a system." And he said, after that, something that seems to me challengingly true. "The

Nazis made use of the worst elements in the ego. The Communists can appeal to what is often the best. That's why Communism is the greater force, incomparably greater. If it used only the evil in men, the danger would be less. It would soon disintegrate. But the good perverted — the right questions, the questions nobody can stop, wrongly answered — that is a formidable thing to deal with!"

"And what can we use in dealing with it, Klaus?"

"Only a greater good," he said. "Only the truth of which Communism is the counterfeit. That is why unless we're accurate we fail."

His friend Gerhardt, who had shared with him three of those prison years, said, "Then what are we speaking of — Communist doctrine or Russian imperialism? Our vocabularies, too, must be accurate!" And we all laughed; for how true, as Tante filling cups observed, that any political discussion today requires at the outset its own dictionary. ("Where I come from," Stephen had earlier said, "it's much safer to be called a libertine than a liberal!") And I pointed out virtuously that at any rate no one had complicated matters by using those words which for most Europeans are now mangled beyond meaning. "Democracy," "freedom," "brotherhood," and the rest of them: words — a bit breezily employed by Americans — that perhaps for a time we should leave unsaid. Living forth what they mean to us as best we can.

Somebody brought in newspapers then. And as Regina read aloud about yesterday's event, I kept saying, "Oh, dear! But it sounds so *different!*" Suddenly shaken; suddenly feeling what it's all too easy for me to feel (for most women to feel, I rather think) — that surely one must stand at a congenital disadvantage! Unfitted to appraise usefully affairs-at-large. In personal relations, in the intimacies of living — here sensibilities are an acknowledged asset; intuitions are honored. With traditional authority one may occupy a salon, a clinic, a bed-chamber. But the world "outside," the issues and policies and maneuvers and machinations — how suddenly esoteric this world can appear! Complex and unapproachable. The pre-serve of experts. Not different in degree, but in very kind.

I sat there listening, feeling suddenly out of it.

For nobody was writing about a Pauli or an Ernst. Or even about the birds, or the song that had so moved me. There were a good many statistics, and some revelatory facts — con-cerning, for instance, the mass disgruntlement apparently to be found: the housing miserably makeshift, it seemed; the food insufficient; and the street "entertainments" pitiably un-festive. It was also reported that the East German youth were in a state of resentment because the delegates from other countries were being fed and accommodated in a superior style. And hundreds of them, thousands — in spite of the rigid police control (at all last stops in the Russian Sector every S-Bahn and U-Bahn compartment was combed) — were managing to swarm over into West Berlin: to look around, to ask questions, to find out, many of them, the pos-sibilities of remaining as refugees. And the West Berliners, with their usual alertness, were picking up groups of the boys and girls; showing them what could be bought in the shops; taking them at night up the lighted Funkturm; buying coffee and cakes for them at the modish cafés on the Kurfürsten-damm, Reception centers, expertly staffed, had been estab-lished; and the American State Department was conducting somewhere a non-stop performance of "true information." (Later, in Munich, at Hildegard's home, I was to meet the man from Washington who had supervised this. "It was one

time," he was to say, "when we really did a first-rate job on
the spot!" — describing the room packed and emptied and
packed again, for session after session; the intense attentive-
ness; the sharp and explicit questions posed.) Two members
of the Bulgarian delegation, it seemed, had already come over,
asking for refuge. And it was expected that during the days
ahead increasing crowds of young people would be making
the same trek: those bearing letters from a responsible person,
a parent or a pastor — vouching for the integrity of their decision to leave — being allowed to remain; but most of them
advised by the authorities to go back: to hold themselves in
readiness for "the right time."

Obviously here was the central story! Not oneself crossing a line, but these swarms of Germans coming this way.
These young people dazzled — according to the accounts —
by the pastries, the automobiles, the scintillating night life;
by all the concrete evidences of a superior system.

"I suppose I ought to stay right here," I said. "And read
the papers!"

But Gerhardt, who hadn't been speaking very much,
abruptly objected. (Gerhardt whose work with the British
authorities involved, one gathered, periodic missions both
secret and hazardous into Eastern territories.) "It's a part,"
he said, "and a significant part. But we make a mistake in
overplaying it like this. Two million people, by the end of
next week, will have been brought into Berlin. Of these, some
thousands will come over here. And of these, in turn, perhaps a third or a half will come over seriously with the idea
of staying." (Later, in talking with staff members at the
reception points, we were to learn that from one third or two
thirds of the boys, and considerably less of the girls, were

found, when interviewed, to have definitely shaped intentions.) "The others," said Gerhardt, "will simply come over, for a variety of reasons. Because they're curious; out of boredom; to pick up what they can. Even, a percentage of them, just to be smart. Two million *could* come, if they were really determined to. A few thousand will."

"But those thousands, Gerhardt — aren't they the hope, the positive element?"

"Yes," he agreed. "And the positive element, on the other side, is those you met yesterday. Those who believe. They too are the few. But it's the few anywhere who represent the real force. If action is decreed, it's they who will take it; and all the rest — the apathetic, the cynical, the confused — they'll fall in behind. As they did under Hitler. As I did myself! We can't bank on people because they grumble about food!" And he quoted the familiar Nietsche passage: "The Germans are always so badly deceived because they try to find a deceiver. If only they have a heady wine for the senses they will put up with bad bread. Intoxication means more to them than nourishment."

"There are those," he said, "who if given a choice between cakes on the Kurfürstendamm and the song you've told us about, would choose the song. That is something that you Americans must learn to understand."

And learn too, I quickly acknowledged, that there could be implicit in such a choice something of tremendous value to the world. "Too many people will settle for the cakes. Perhaps we need those who're prepared to do without them so that the song may become a true song."

Regina read aloud then something else — a bit about the British delegation. They were being, it appeared, housed for the two weeks in the Karlshorst headquarters of the Russian

Administration and the Russian Army: a spot understandably unbeloved by the more apprehensive East Berliners. And here, as soon as they had settled in, in their blazers and voiles, they had proceeded, without asking anyone's permission, quite casually apparently, with an Alice in Wonderland matter-of-factness, to take down from the walls of the rooms assigned to them all the slogans and posters and pictures of Stalin that had been militantly set forth.

"Those British!" exclaimed Tante, throwing up her hands.

Whoever else would have come, and then promptly done that!

"But it's typical!" I said, as we all laughed. "It's so exactly like them!"

And Klaus reminded us of the story related by Silone: of how, at a top-level international conclave of Party members, when a certain insidious course of action was prescribed, the English delegate had stood up and protestingly pointed out, "But that would be lying!" — a joke speeded, it was said, all the way up to Marshal Stalin!

"There you have it!" said Klaus (who had been at Oxford). "And that's why Americans who think the British are 'going Communist' understand neither Communism nor the British!"

And I was reminded, in turn, of a newsreel I'd seen at a London cinema with another German friend, a political refugee — before the war this was, in 1939. Somewhere or other in the East End, Sir Oswald Moseley had been parading with his Black Shirts; and the audience had sat passive before the braggart-sight until suddenly, in the film, a dockhand casually standing at the curb had turned towards the camera — all Puck in his grin — and given a wink that was like the confidential sign, easy and intimate, used in a family. It had been as if he were saying, "Crikey! wot a bloke!" and instantly the whole audience had burst out laughing! The German, I remembered, had observed with satisfaction, "They'll never make Fascists out of these English! Such people would always, at the wrong moment, be amused!"

Gerhardt asked me if I knew a statement of Goethe's: "By nothing do men show their character more than by the things they laugh at."

And Regina said, "We Berliners laugh ironically — at what we hate. The English laugh kindly — at what they love."

"I think that we need both kinds," I said.

And thought how valuable they were, these people. Who had come so painful, so difficult a way, and stood now on this hazardous front — stood for all of us, not just themselves — well knowing that if suddenly the wall were to break they would be among the first to pay with their lives.

Later in the morning I went back across the line.

And here it all was again. Alexanderplatz. The dense and slow-milling hordes in blue shirts; the music from loud-speakers — intermittently giving place to thunderous phrases that seemed uttered by a giant in the sky. Here again were the lyricism and the violence of the posters; the little stalls, the trivial merchandise (bits of soap, knitted caps, stickpin doves made of metal) — all looking, after the grandiose achievement of yesterday, even shabbier than before; more inchoate, more nondescript; more than ever like the raw material for something.

The Berolinahaus directly faces the S-Bahn — no distance at all; but I found myself, as I started to shove a way towards it, helplessly caught up in a whirl of children. Small boys and girls, all wanting one to scribble in their autograph books and, after that, to sign something else: a long scroll at another and more prominent booth, with a sign that read "Grüss-Adresse an J. V. Stalin Zeichnet Eüch ein!" "Stalin! Stalin!" the children all cried, shining with excitement, beaming up. If one had been alone with them in a quiet field and had asked, "Who is Stalin?" what would they have said? There was a steady procession of signers past the stall. And now, as one watched, a blond young woman, holding in her arms a child who couldn't have been more than two, was putting into his hand the pencil given her. Firmly she folded his fingers around it: the guided signature of a baby, sending greetings to Moscow. And now a trio of teen-agers, with their braided hair bound about their small heads in that charmingly simple Mädchen fashion; and, after them, another swarm of little boys with badges on their shirts and caps clapped on anyhow, and grubby knees and flushed cheeks like little boys anywhere. A young man with one leg was supervising it all. He was using his crutch as dexterously as a limb; and he belonged, one judged, to that particular generation (roughly from the late twenties to the middle thirties) which had — on that first exploration with Friedl — struck me as being somehow especially critical. The precarious age-group. Or the group, rather, in which the elements of unrest seemed to pulse like a nerve closest to the surface. And how understandably! When one stopped to think. For the younger ones, the student class so often met with, were the heirs of a debacle; as adolescents they had experienced the explosion of a myth. But these others, the generation of this young man — it was they who had come of age with the full dazzlement of that myth. They had had mapped out for them (if going with the tide) how secure,

how privileged a role in their world! With life at their heels
and the future theirs, they had belonged to a fraternity of
supermen: seeing, out ahead, a course fixed bright for a
thousand years.

And dreams die hard. Do we half remember? The false
and the perverted, as well as the true. And when once a
human being has said to himself, however darkly and cruelly
at the expense of others, "I count for something! I matter
in the world!" — how impossible to suppress that stir in the
mind. And how vulnerable he will prove (if left without a
valid concept of himself) to the next phantasy riding the air.

Klaus and Gerhardt were of this generation. By way of an
ordeal they had found themselves. Through the long inward-
ness of those Russian years, each had achieved, in his own
terms, clarity, certainty, precision of purpose. "It's ironic, I
suppose," Klaus had said earlier, "that it was in Russia, where
God is officially denied, that I was provided with the *space* in
which to find faith!" And he had spoken of how Rilke, the
poet he loved, had turned with hope to the idea of those vasty
regions to the east. "In Germany, one had no room to think
in. Nowhere to go. For those first months in Russia I knew,
for the first time, a kind of glacial emptiness. As far as one
could look, there was nothing to lay hold on. It was the end
or the beginning. And it became quite simple. Either one
must matter, right there, like that — in one's own soul and
before God — or not at all. Not as an officer of the German
Army; not even as a German. It was reaching some common
denominator as man. When they captured me," he had said,
"I was already in bonds. While still a prisoner, I found I
could be free."

The young man on the crutch stood there at the booth. The

music vehemently flared about him and, when it halted, at once the giant voice occupied the air. "Youth of the World — " "Freedom, Unity, the Strength of the People — "

"No room to think in," Klaus had said.

And I thought of another and different voice: of Hans' at Berchtesgaden — and climbing with him in the cold and brilliant night with the mountains all about us moonstruck, massive, in immensities of space, and the words ringing out like a kind of song, "We hold these truths to be self-evident, that all men are created equal: that they are endowed by their Creator with certain inalienable rights — "

All men. Or no one at all.

And I wanted to say aloud, "*You too! you too!*" — to the young man, to the children, to everyone here.

Eventually the inside of the building was reached; and here, in the Presse room, crowded and noisy as it had been before, I found almost at once (although Käthe was the one I was actually looking for) the other girl, Liesl.

"Hullo! Hullo — " she was calling out. And when I made my way over to her she asked, with eagerness, "Did you see it all yesterday? Was it wonderful to watch?"

She was stationed at the circular information desk, at the section marked "English"; and she was as sunny, as warm, as delighted to greet one as she had been upstairs when previously encountered. "I *hoped* you'd come back! And here you are! — just in time." For she was, it appeared, about to leave for lunch. And when she asked, a bit diffidently, if I would have it with her, I said, "But I'd love to! How nice of you to ask me."

At the same moment two Frenchmen emerging from the melee paused at the desk. They requested, in English, some sort of information; and when Liesl asked them what papers they represented, they each gave the name of a Paris journal.

"Oh!" she said, charmed, "are you *French?*" and at once pointed out, "But you know, we have French interpreters too! Look, down there!" — pleased as punch it was obvious that such courtesies had been thought of: that all these friends were so well embraced!

"They seem to be doing fine in English!" I observed; for the elder of them at least spoke it admirably. A man with an intelligent and sensitive face: the face, certainly, of one with his wits habitually about him.

"That's because I lived for several years in America."

"You did?" And while Liesl wrote something down, I said, "I wonder why I never seem to think of Frenchmen living anywhere but in France!"

"Well, we don't normally! Not unless we're obliged to. The insular English explore the earth; the cosmopolitan Frenchman prefers his own square mile!"

We laughed. And I asked, "Where were you in America?"

"The British Zone," he said.

The information was given to them; they disappeared; it was a full three minutes before I thought, "What was that?" The words had been uttered quite clearly and sensibly; they had *sounded* sensible. And one thought, "Good heavens! is this what happens!" Would one, if left long enough in this air, begin to talk gibberish and not even notice it!

Across the table, in the restaurant to which she had brought us, Liesl lifted her Apfelsaft. "Freundschaft!" she said. We drank to friendship. And she said, "How happy I am that you are here! How good it is, isn't it, for all people to be friends?"

"If they are true friends, yes," I said.

"It should be so everywhere, everywhere in the world!"

"But it can't be, can it, until something happens? People can't be friends if they're kept apart."

"Ah, yes. That is so. That is why our Festival means so much!" And she said, "If only all could have come — all who believe as we do in peace."

She was charming to watch, with that eagerness in her face, that candid delight in an unprecedented windfall — for she hadn't, I'd soon learned, ever personally talked with an American before; it was years, apparently, since she had even encountered one. A G.I. long ago had once given her some chocolate. "But it is different now; the Western police will let no one come. If they try to reach us, often they are hurt." She kept reminding me, as she sat there saying such things, of someone else, someone recently experienced. Pauli — that was it. Physically, of course, they were two of a kind, fair-haired and blue-eyed and belonging out-of-doors, with that fresh glisten to them, that look at the same time radiant and blank, like the blind shine on water or glass. There was the same impulsive friendliness too, guileless and beguiling as a child's gift. There was the same almost pathological "innocence."

"Liesl, may I ask you something I've been wondering?"

"Oh, please!" she said. "I should like us to talk about many things!"

"Well, you spoke the other day — remember? — about churches. You go to a church? You believe in Christianity?"

"Oh, yes! And you?"

"Yes, I too. But what I wonder is this. How can what is going on over here be acceptable to a Christian?"

Her gaze, across the table, was unflinchingly frank. "Please?" she said.

After a moment I asked, "What does it mean to you, Christianity?"

"Oh, *peace*," she said, "peace in the world, and all men living together as brothers. That is what everybody must work for, isn't it?"

"But if that is so, how can the hatred be accepted?"

It was as if some kind of flow had been slowed. Or as if she were having to play back the words, like words spoken in an unfamiliar accent.

"For instance," I said, "these horrible posters."

"Posters — " she repeated. Again like a test. And then quickly, eagerly, with manifest relief, "But our posters are *beautiful!* All the youth of the world — "

"Yes, I know. There are those, the beautiful ones. But the others, I mean. The hate ones against the country I come from."

It was several moments before she found her way to an answer. When she did, she spoke with a kind of dismay, as if a child, unfairly dealt with, were saying, "But our Festival — you have *seen* what our Festival is! How all have come to it! All are welcome — "

"Oh, *Liesl!*" I said.

Later, with Käthe, there was to be the concrete thing: the avowed position and the mobilized arguments — something realistically to come to grips with; so perhaps now, with this other girl, it was the very transparency of what she was, the lack of guile even starker than the lack of truth, that pitched one suddenly into a kind of hopelessness. Here she sat, with her wide eyes. Not far away. Not out of reach. Not a nameless cipher behind an Iron Curtain. Facing each other, we were sharing the same meal. And yet what could one say? How could a drift of lies be addressed? It was as if one were confronted by a soft blur, a mentality that would dissolve at any point touched. It was as if there were nothing whatever to be done. Or nothing short of an outright blow. "Liesl, you're the dupe of something monstrous!" — that could be said, the simple truth; but what earthly good would the saying of it do? In turn, and probably with tears, she would exclaim, "Oh, it is terrible what they teach them in the West! I met an American I liked so much, I thought we were friends; but it is so, it is true, what we are told! She believed the most dreadful things about us — "

How could one speak to the indoctrinated mind?

Suddenly I wanted to get up and go away. It seemed too much, too frightening a thing: this immensity and density of misunderstanding, this towering force of falsehood in the world. One wanted to get away — which was all very well! But where? and what good would that do either? This place could be gone from easily enough; but the place itself, here it would remain. Liesl would remain. And Pauli. And Ernst. And how many others like, or unlike, them? And one would know; the knowledge would be fixed in one's heart. Wherever one was, there it would be too.

Once I wrote something down for myself.

> "Come you away, away," they cry,
> "world is too bitter
> for heart to bear."

The singing is sweeter
than all of birds
singing together:
the words
are the sweetest words on air;
no other spell can half compare
with the secret call.

"Come you away

away

away — "

But where? Where
is there left to flee?
Where are the lovely innocent lands,
the luminous isles?
World has grown stern;
there is nowhere to turn
in fantasy,
nowhere at all.
Self must drop of its own
despair
or lift free
just where it stands.

Well, here it was, in East Berlin. And for quantities of other people, who couldn't be choosy, it would have to go on being East Berlin. Everybody couldn't be a refugee; half a country — or half Europe — couldn't be evacuated.

And suddenly something seemed of piercing importance. If what one believed to be essential truth *was* true, then it was true *here*. To be acted upon as one would act upon it anywhere else: with faith, not in oneself, but in it. Liesl, sitting here, supposed us to be friends. And what was the fact? What did one set against her assumption — denial, which would destroy? or an altogether different order of affirmation?

It seemed, suddenly, a choice involving the whole shape of life. And one wanted to say aloud (not only to Liesl), "Yes there is a point at which we are friends!" For surely that point must always exist. Call it what one will — some inmost identity; some "inalienable right" to conscience, reason, reality of being — surely it exists as literally, as ineffaceably as the mathematical fact behind the juggled figures. If a man were no more than the sum of his misconceptions, then in truth we were doomed, and why make any bones about it? But that wasn't — that never had been — what one believed. Anywhere at all. Here was a girl with a headful of lies. But one wasn't addressing *them*, one was addressing *her*.

One could say, ruthlessly, "The posters are outside; come along with me, and I'll show them to you! I'll force you to acknowledge them!" One could drive the lie in. But I remembered Herta. I remembered her looking me straight in the eye and saying in a voice clear as a bell, "You know I never knew anything about them — that I never dreamed such things could be!" Concentration camps it had been that time: the same concentration camps that Herta, in London, before the war, had wept shocked tears over (real tears, I saw them) after reading an authoritative series of articles in an English journal. And I remembered something else, related to me by Hildegard: how once she had been in the vicinity of Dachau and had seen on a road, herded between guards, a pitiful procession of human beings, and how she had rushed and knocked on several doors, telling people she knew, "You say you've never seen proof of such things; then come quickly! come and look for yourselves!" And how no one had gone. No one had "been able to leave" just then.

"It isn't *lying*," I had said. "I can grasp that now. It's something much deeper than telling a lie. It's the *will to be unaware* — that's it, isn't it?" And here in Berlin, Klaus, in speaking of the same thing had said, "In a way, of course, a tragic way, it's the mark of our morality. Other people see the Germans without a sense of guilt. But our guilt is unbearable to us — that is why it is driven inward and becomes, as you have seen, a kind of sickness of the soul. We deny it, not because it seems to us slight, but because the enormity of it is something that we don't know how to face." And he had said, "This is the country, after all, that gave to the world Luther's Bible. And a people out of whom such a light came can't betray it *admittedly* — not unless they're madmen. The betrayal itself, if it's to succeed, must be given holiness!"

Liesl hadn't said, "Oh, well, they're only posters — " or, "Yes, I know; they worry me too; but they aren't, of course, the important part — " She hadn't sought to excuse them; she'd denied their existence. Almost as if she were saying in panic before a threat, "Oh, please, don't! Don't force me to look! Leave me with the friendship, the flowers, the songs!"

"Because the enormity of it," Klaus had said, "is something that we don't know how to face."

"And what is the answer, Klaus? How can guilt be exorcised?"

"The answer is always the same, isn't it?"

"Love, you mean."

"But love of a certain kind," he had said. "Not sentimental love! That's worse, if anything, than the condemnation. We Germans are soft — spongy — with that!"

I had thought of the word that Peter used, in speaking of

this country at the refugee camp. "A *tough* kind of love."
That wounded, if it must, in order to heal.

"Yes," Klaus had said. "A love that can strike unsparingly
at the sin, while freeing the man."

It was as if Liesl, as she sat here, were saying, "Oh, *please*
— *please don't!*" The precariousness of her security pitifully
laid bare. Or not pitifully! one realized. For here was the
hope. Here in the very immediateness of her dismay. And one
wanted to say back to her, "Oh, Liesl, you'll lose nothing!
Nothing true will be forfcited by facing the false. The world
will be a harder, a more adult place, but an imcomparably
more rewarding one. And you won't be left friendless — never
fear that! Outside, in this other life that awaits you, there's a
company of companions far truer than anything you've ever
known."

Instead of which I said, "I'm glad, Liesl, that you care like
this — about peace and brotherhood and all these things;
because I do too; I care very much. And so perhaps if we talk
together about what we believe we can help each other, and
be of more use in this difficult world. For I know that you
want to be, as truly as I do."

V

Every conversation that took place over here was to move with
a kind of delicacy into its own shape. There was no formula
of rebuttal; at least none that I was to find. However stereotyped and inflexible, however wearisomely identical the argu-

ments dished out, each time one had to come freshly to the individual. And each time, if there was a yielding on the other side, it was at a point that one couldn't have determined beforehand: at some doubt inadvertently or unconsciously disclosed; at some outleak of concern or involuntary enquiry that had to be waited for and, when it came, handled with lightness, not made too much of; because one wasn't here to triumph over anybody else.

There was no formula that one could see. But one soon began to feel out what was effective. Such as letting the other person have the first say.

This seemed to me, from the start, only sensible — in view of the fact that from the other side I was the misinformed and misguided one; the one who needed to be straightened out. And since we were meeting on his territory, not mine, one could at least extend the courtesy of saying, in effect, "Very well, go ahead. Show me what you believe. Here's your chance to make a convert, so let's see what you can produce!" There was, too, the further fact (surely to be taken sympathetically into account) that these young people lived constantly at the point *of being told*. They were blared at; bossed; maneuvered about. And so again in terms of plain common sense, wasn't it much better for them to be allowed, for a change, to hold forth themselves: to get off their chests whatever they wanted to — even if it was only what they'd had pumped into them — and to be allowed to do so as lengthily as they pleased, without challenge or interruption; the floor theirs? This took, admittedly, a bit of doing on one's own part! When every instinct was to hit back hard and fast at the first whopper launched into the air. "That's a damnable lie!" one naturally wanted to say; but to do so, at any rate early in a conversation, was at once to forfeit, one very soon found, the only atmosphere in which a contact could validly be made. (Not to mention the manifest impossibility of attempting to refute, detail by detail, a cloudy complex of fables, perversions, and fears.) Indignation, however righteous, simply didn't pay off. It was unstrategic; from the word go. Whereas patience had certain immediate advantages. In the first place, by showing that one was willing to listen, one invited in return the courtesy of being listened to. And in the second place, by letting someone else go first one was often able to detect in what was said an emphasis, or an omission, that could be an inkling of some point of vulnerability or receptiveness. There was also, of course, the commonplace fact that anyone allowed to go on and on, without evoking either agreement or dissent, is bound to experience a gradual deflating of initial enthusiasm. There's a point at which intervention becomes positively welcome! If only for the sake of regalvanizing matters!

So one learned to let the other person speak first. To be patient; to be relaxed; to quell in oneself not only anger but that tension so familiar when something is at stake and that can, without a word, communicate itself, creating at once a corresponding tension. There was a kind of *lightness* that was invaluable, one found; although lightness perhaps isn't quite the word. But again and again, at moments when the contact seemed about to break, with two people flying apart into clenched camps, something was saved by being loosed into the air — as if it hardly mattered, or mattered in such a way that one didn't choose to make of it a clumsy quarrel.

For what one realized, of course, almost from the start, was that mere argument could settle nothing. Facts could be militantly pitched against fictions; but what was that? — one's own word against the word of Authority; and why, it could logically enough be asked, should someone who had dropped in out of the blue expect to be believed, on the basis of words? Each side could assert with equal force, "That is a lie!" Each could roll out its respective "evidence." And one was dealing (again it had to be remembered) with people who had been for the past twenty years — which meant for practically the whole of their lives — subjected to onslaught after onslaught of "evidence"; so that in a way the more fluent and aggressive the presentation of one's case, the more suspect it could seem: smacking of the well-oiled machinations of the West!

Not that facts were a negligible asset; far from it. In a sense they were the very bone and sinew of one's position. But there was, one realized, something that each time counted ahead of them. Not a case; not an argument; certainly not an abstract declaration of principles. But *an attitude towards life.* This was what registered.

For this, one was to learn, was the "different" thing. The one factor for which, on the opposite side, there appeared to be no fixed pattern of retort. There was also, of course, no way in which the effect of it could be precisely gauged; which meant that one had to act on faith, trusting the validity of the attitude itself. And such action obviously involved, to begin with, being prepared at all costs to stick to the truth. Even if this obliged one to relinquish ground; to say, "Yes, there you have a point," or, "I'm sorry, but I don't know the answer to that." When Käthe, for instance, was to plunge into a comparison of the economies of Eastern and Western Germany, it was necessary (since such, alas, is the fact) to say, "Käthe, I'm a perfect dunce at economics! If I pretended otherwise, it would be sheer hypocrisy. So whatever your point — I'll have to concede it! Whether an *expert* would, is another matter! But me, I'm simply not qualified to judge." Just as it was necessary to say to Ernst, when he recounted in detail the Scottsboro Case (a bit garbled, considerably heightened, but essentially accurate), "Yes, that's true. And don't think any American's proud of it either!"

This was how one would normally talk. Acknowledging, without any sense of fatality — any cataclysmic central collapse! — the fallibility of either person or system. And it was this very thing, one was soon to perceive, this easy, unfearful relationship to the truth — allowing one to admit to a failing or a flaw and even on occasion to draw attention to it — that constituted over here in talking with these young people a tremendous advantage. Each side could lay claim to a monolithic absoluteness; each could accuse the other of total iniquity. This was the established pattern of procedure; this they were both drilled in and prepared to meet with. But if, instead, one said to them, "Yes, there you have a point — " or "That's something, frankly, I'm not properly informed about — " letting it be seen that one attached to the admission no embarrassment, no stigma, and certainly no threat to the true substance of one's cause; if one could laugh; if one could lightly loose into the air a moment about to tighten hard as a fist — then suddenly the advantage could be one's own.

For it was as if, standing at some point of security — a point not dependent upon "advantages" at all — one could afford a leeway denied to the others. It wasn't that the seriousness of anything was blurred; by lightening them, one was in no way trivializing these issues. It was simply some kind of inner refusal to be imposed upon by a ponderous miscalculation. Here was a world in which it was being said, over and over by a giant voice, "Two and two put together make three or five — " Or every now and then (if convenient) even four!

That one's own sums could all too often be awry was, heaven knew, an indisputable fact. And in the world one came from, how frequent and sobering the mistakes chalked up, how painfully the false deductions had to be erased. But at any rate there existed a fixed premise. However imperfect the mathematicians themselves, the principles of mathematics stood fast. Everyone on earth could muddle the rules; but the rules remained. This was the point. This was the security within the mist. And once it was seen, a kind of ease could be experienced — a kind of relaxation in the thick of the fray that wasn't a washing of the hands of anything, but the acknowledgment of a force at work in the universe and therefore a factor in the immediate situation. Two and two didn't need — in order to make four — one's own harried protestations. They didn't even, in a sense, need one's agreement. The fact simply was; it existed; it was here. If one failed to utilize it, the loss was one's own. And if one could help to communicate this, to say, "I've found, in the life I know, that this works and this and the results are such-and-so — " then that, obviously, was a sound and indeed imperative contribution. But one wasn't responsible for the fact's own force. One bore witness; as best one could. And if this involved the defeat of something else, it was neither a personal victory for oneself nor a personal ignominy for the other side: it was the potency in the truth, in the light itself, that challenged or unsettled or disposed of the darkness. And perhaps — who knew? — in that delicate and hazardous place called consciousness, measurable by no instrument as yet devised, it would, in the end, be the imponderables that tipped the unseen scales. Perhaps, in the end, the finger-touch could outweigh the bludgeon blow. . . .

At any rate, for oneself an approach was evolved that seemed

to make sense. It was playing by ear; not a platform performance; and there was nothing to show for it but a handful of
gestures, the turn of a voice, the look on a face. And the feeling within oneself which grew stronger with each contact that
however bewilderingly difficult the job, there was nothing
here absolutely unredeemable. The tools, or tactics, in one's
own particular case seemed to be patience, a light hand, dead
honesty; the use of laughter, and a holding fast to the conviction that there exist in life certain basic truths which, if true,
are impersonal, timeless, unlocalized and indestructible; and
inalienably the right of every man on earth. This, and being
prepared to respect the other's motive. Or at any rate being
prepared to say openly, "I will start by assuming that you, too,
care as much as I do about the things that mean to us a good
life. And in return I expect you to believe the same of me."

For wasn't this the truth? Wasn't there among these young
people encountered, however perverted their concepts and
their course, the desire for the very things that were dinned
into the air night and day? *Peace — fellowship — unity —
joy.* The sound of the words was so revoltingly false, so cruel
a travesty to one's own ear, that it had to be remembered time
and again that the words themselves wouldn't be used unless
it was recognized, by the manipulating power, that they be-
spoke the actual longing of the heart. Like the friendship
song, they must be salvaged, redeemed. They must be made
true. Not beaten out.

In talking with, or rather listening to, someone like Liesl,
the usual pattern of argument was produced: in her instance
at a level of such unrelieved naïveté that one had to come in
on it as one would with a child, gently, and not attempting
to do much more than say, "Ah, but listen to this! This is

something that I happen to know about myself, and you'll be
so happy to hear of it, Liesl, because it is — isn't it? — the
way you, too, want things to be."

In this basic pattern the world was two worlds. Perilously,
grievously, and implacably so. In one of them was something
called "the people," altruistically championed by the Soviet
Union; and, in the other, there were people too—but people
victimized and misguided by a dire conspiracy of false leadership. Swap the names, and the view was one's own. There were
even the same phrases, the same assurance brought forth. "We
know it isn't the *people* of America who are our enemies; the
people everywhere want to be friends; it's those who tell them
such wicked lies." For the Soviet Union itself one could detect no actual spontaneity of feeling. In spite of the beneficent
role assigned to it, and in spite of the poster-and-proclamation
emphasis upon the person of Stalin, this was something that
struck one at every turn. Even the heart of Käthe, one was to
infer, didn't beat for Russia. For an idea, yes; for a cause and
a campaign; but not literally for another country, or for the
Kremlin, or even the Politburo. Which left one with the
feeling time and again that the tinderbox of emotion was still
marked "Germany." Or with the impression, at any rate,
among many of those talked with, that this fluent conversion
to a different faith could, if the tune were changed in the air,
revert overnight (at some level of instinct exploited, not ex-
punged, by the present influence) to a doctrine again addressing itself to "the blood."

The shift *between* myths could be a two-way thing. Only
the move *out* was decisive, one realized. And if at some point
the tune were to change, or the faith were to be jarred (there
was Käthe with the Jewish father she had lost; Liesl with that
flinching at-all-costs from violence) — where was there to go?

what was there to believe? If Ernst were suddenly, in the course of events, to find himself at a point of inner conflict, in which direction would he proceed to move? Where was it being made *possible* for him to move?

"The people," one gathered — in this basic pattern — occupied a somewhat paradoxical position. The happy beneficiaries of democracy, fraternity, and incontestable power, they were, simultaneously, the threatened, the ill-done-by, the perfidiously attacked. Just as the Soviet Union itself existed, it appeared, at a point compounded at one and the same time of supreme potency and maximum peril. Ostensibly it was the first that charged the air; actually, one was soon enough to find, it was the second — the peril — that emerged in conversations as the dominant theme. Actually, indeed, it underlay and overlay everything else. It was the "reason," the "explanation," perpetually at hand; it motivated, shaped, and concretely justified every step of a course. There wasn't an act, or an aspect of the order — however temporarily infelicitous! — that couldn't at once be rendered "legitimate" in the light of this ceaseless, inexorable *threat*.

In one way it had a curiously familiar sound! For how dominated by negatives one's own air could seem: how riddled with mistrust, slander, fear — even (at levels below responsible policy) with the delibcrate, unscrupulous exploiting of that fear. Under the same insistent sense of threat, how frighteningly submissive people were becoming — people one knew, nice people, good people — to the open encroachment of the very attitudes and methods of which the enemy himself was a past master. How familiar — and how profound beyond words the difference!

For what one was piercingly to realize here was a momentous fact.

However imperfect the society one came from, however disheartingly and even dangerously confused, there existed within it, within the Western tradition, not only the possibility but the natural assumption of a certain order of life: an order that could somehow, at the expense of none, develop logically to the advantage of all. Say it was still an unrealized idea; say it was betrayed, time and again, and beset by reverses so numerous and complicated that repeatedly its proponents were open to both charges of hypocrisy from without and the recognition within of grave failure. Say the worst that could be said — nevertheless there it was. The ideal, fallen short of, was still confidently held. So that it was natural, from where one stood, to conceive of a world in which all official judgments and acts weren't determined, automatically, by the existence of an absolute, pre-ordained foe.

One's own air was troubled enough, that was true; fear and suspicion were poisonously infecting it. But if suddenly that outside menace were to evaporate, surely life — going on — would be substantially the same. Certain drastic adjustments would have to be made, economically and politically; certain groups, to be sure, both left and right, would find themselves all at once dangling at loose ends. But what heads would roll? What basic propositions would be disastrously invalidated? If the friendship — the "Freundschaft!" — so shouted about here were in truth to become a living fact, obviously it would hardly spell for the West instant catastrophe! Whereas in this other, this misconceived world —

It was this that suddenly was to strike the mind. If the enmity were gone, what would happen here? For the threat was needed. Wasn't that the whole point? Danger from without (or the illusion of it) wasn't something peripheral, a phenomenon inadvertently and unfortunately incurred; it was built into the very thrust and structure of this thing; so intrinsic, so inseparable from a central thesis that it could no more be removed without an inmost collapse than could the steel girders from a Manhattan skyscraper. Without fear, without the bogey of a ready-to-pounce foe, what on earth would there be to "justify," to "vindicate" a regime? How otherwise could they even temporarily succeed — these strategies and techniques upon which an entrenched group must depend for the preservation of its very existence?

It was in Berlin that one realized something for the first time.

However imperfect the society one came from, it didn't require a devil in order to *be*.

Sitting opposite her, in the restaurant, it was easy enough to perceive in the girl Liesl the point at which she herself was most vulnerable. When she said "peace," she almost desperately meant it — or meant, at any rate, the absence of war. In that terrible finale of a city's ordeal, she had, one was to learn, been trapped under a building for many hours with a dead child, mangled and staring, beside her. The reference was only a momentary one: a nightmare, one realized — to be thrust back blindly behind doors and doors. When she said, "We must never, never have war! That is why our Festival means so much — all of us together believing in peace — " it was something to be dealt with, not clinically, with facts, but from one's own heart, one's own concern. And what counted seemed essentially to be what was *meant*; not the words spoken (for they could sound, as uttered, hopelessly kindergarten in a giant world) but the impulse itself — the desire to touch through.

For at least one could say, "Liesl, I know what you're told

over here. You believe, don't you, that the people I come from are plotting against you — even arming for war the other half of your own Germany? The danger, you believe, comes from us. That's what you're told, and so you believe it. And perhaps, if I were you, knowing nothing else, I'd think the same thing. But you see, I happen to come from the West. I know what it's like. I'm part of that world — " (A point, one soon learned, it was advisable to hammer in, saying, "I'm a perfectly ordinary American, not different in the least; there are quantities of us, millions, who believe these things!" — since the tendency, one found, if confidence was established, was to waft one aloft as a seraphic exception: absolved from the complicity one's compatriots were caught in!) "I'm part of that world, and so I know what it's like. I know what kind of speeches are being given, and what's written in newspapers — good and bad — and what people are saying among themselves. And Liesl, it isn't the way you suppose! If only you could come to America yourself, or to England, or even to the rest of Europe, you'd realize this. You wouldn't have to believe what anyone told you. You could decide for yourself. Just as I — coming here and listening to your side — must decide for myself. If you could come and meet us and see us for what we are — "

"But it isn't — Oh, it isn't *the people* — " she said.

"All right then, the leaders. But you see, they too aren't as you suppose. I've talked with some of our leaders, Liesl. It's quite possible to, you know — they don't shut themselves off, behind guns, in a fortress! After all, we elect them; we choose them ourselves — they come from ourselves, and sometimes, after they've been leaders for a while, they deliberately go back to being ordinary citizens, lawyers or whatever they were before, like anybody else, like all the rest of us. You see, it's such a different concept of leadership — "

And unpremeditatedly, even somewhat to my own surprise for I hadn't for ages so much as thought of it, I found myself telling her about President Harding and how once — a misguided David in a pink cotton dress — I'd very nearly slain him, by mistake, with a golf ball. (This being another of the points soon recognized: the advisability of talking, not in abstractions, but in terms of things that had really happened: letting all sorts of incidents fly out, just as they came, striking off their own sense.) So, "Once," I said, "when I was a little girl, we went to live in Washington, and almost every morning early before breakfast my father used to play golf for an hour. The President of the United States did the same. At the same place. And he was, incidentally, one of our dud Presidents. They vary, you know — the way people do. But anyhow, there we were on the green — for my brother and I used to be allowed to go along; we'd carry the golf clubs; 'caddying' it's called. And one morning, feeling bored at just standing and watching, I popped down a ball and took a wallop at it myself — " Away it had sailed, gratifyingly fast: missing by a hairsbreadth the Presidential brow. There had been, I remembered, a bit of a stir. Several gentlemen had come up and said, "*Little girl!*" And I'd felt, on the whole, rather pleased with myself — it being the first time (as a well-brought-up child) that I'd sensationally occupied the center of a stage.

"So you see," I said, "our leaders are really quite in the open! If even a little girl can almost knock one out!"

For a moment I didn't understand Liesl's face. Not until she asked, "But what *happened* to you!"

"Nothing," I said. "Nothing happened to me, Liesl. I was

told, of course, to be more careful. But you see what I mean; it's such a different way, somehow, of having leaders. That's why the things that are said over here — they don't make sense, if one knows what it's like. But then I suppose that's bound to be the case, isn't it? The difference between knowing something, and only hearing about it from others. For instance — " We were eating meat and salad and potatoes: well cooked and satisfactorily served. "For instance, I was told that the food over here was frightfully bad. Everybody said so! But it isn't, is it? Or not this meal, anyhow. Is this typical, would you say — what we're having here?"

Her anxiety, her eagerness to gain a point, were somehow moving. "Oh, yes, truly! Our people all have enough to eat now; it is not as it was. Anyone will tell you!"

(Which I found, at that particular time, to be so.)

"Then I'll tell them that. It helps to know the truth. And what do you hear about their food, I wonder?"

After a moment she said, "Many people in Western Germany are without food; it is hard, very hard for them."

"That's what you hear? Well — it just goes to show, doesn't it!"

After another pause she asked, "You have been in Western Germany?"

"Oh, yes. All over it. In each of the Zones."

"But you stay with Americans?"

With those living iniquitously off the fat of the land!

"As a matter of fact, no. I've been staying everywhere with German friends. I don't happen to know any Americans in Germany. Except Peter," I appended; and found myself telling her, in some detail, about Peter. "You'd like him, I think. He cares tremendously about all these things — peace, and people learning to understand one another; all the things that

you, too, care about, Liesl." I explained how he was working
in a refugee camp; how he'd given up his job in America to
come here, because he wanted to be of help and to learn,
realistically, what could be done by ordinary people to bring
about in the world a better state of affairs. "I've just been
staying with him, at the camp in Bremen. I was there last
week. So I saw it for myself. And I met and talked with the
refugees — all kinds of people they are, of course; those forced
to leave their homes by what the Russians have done; and
those who lost everything they had under Hitler. And still
others, of course, who've escaped from here. From Eastern
Germany. You know, don't you, that people are all the time
crossing over to us?"

"Oh, no!" she said. "That isn't so!" And she said, "It is
here they come, to us! — only they aren't permitted to! The
Western police *shoot* them — especially the Negroes!" Something like horror came into her voice. "They kill them!" she
said. "It is dreadful — dreadful — "

"Liesl, listen to me! Have you ever met anyone who's come
over here?"

"Oh, yes! he spoke to us! He told us how it is!"

"He?" I said. "One person?"

There was a point, one was to find, in almost every conversation when the same thing had to be said. The form, and
the tone, could each time vary; but essentially it was the same;
for what else was there to say?

"Liesl, you'll have to decide, won't you? Because what I'm
telling you isn't what you've been told. It isn't only different,
it's almost the exact opposite. And in a way I can't help you;
I realize that. It's up to you — you yourself must choose. Am
I telling the truth; or am I telling lies? It's one or the other;
it can't be both." For one could sense, sometimes, a sudden

blind scurry at some under-level of thought: as if an effort were being made to reconcile contradictions. "I'm telling the truth, or I'm telling lies; and it's for you to decide in your own mind. Here I am, right here and quite real! You can listen to my voice and watch my face, and ask me anything you wish to ask. And I'll answer you with what I know myself to be true; but I can't do more. I can't believe for you." And one could say, too, "If you choose not to believe me, that's your concern. It won't alter the facts, or change the way I think. It's you, not I, who will lose or gain by the choice made."

But one couldn't (this too one each time found) let it end quite there. Not at the point of another's confusion. For how graceless a thing — to sow consternation, and nothing else. Each time there was a statement of faith to be made: to oneself, I suppose, as much as to Liesl or whoever it might be.

"I believe that all of us have to decide, in much the same way. We're told this and we're told that, from the moment we're born, and it can look, can't it, a bewildering sort of mess? With no solid point from which to appraise. But I believe something else; I truly believe it — it seems to me the central fact for us all. If, in our heart — at the very core of ourselves — we want more than anything to know the truth, if we're *willing* to know it, at whatever the cost to our own pride or however difficult it may be to change our opinions — or to step out alone, or to face danger — if that desire is really there, then I believe that somehow the truth will be recognized. I believe it is a kind of divine right. Belonging to all men. Wherever they are. To you, Liesl, in East Berlin. To me in America. Equally and justly; almost like the sun. If I didn't believe that, I don't think it would be decent for me to be here at all, or to be talking with you like this; it wouldn't be fair."

And with Liesl there was something else to be said. Returning to the Berolinahaus we passed on the street, and close at hand, a glare of posters. Neither of us looked at them, or spoke a word. But when we were back in the crowded Presse room, and I was thanking her for her courtesy in taking me to lunch, I said, "Liesl, if you happen at any time to see those posters — the ones I spoke of, the ugly ones — will you remember something? Will you remember it's the country I come from? I'd appreciate that."

VI

With Käthe, of course, the proposition was a different one.

There was still another hour before Ernst was due; and so here we were, on a bench against the wall. When I'd said, after finding her, "Oh, Käthe — could we *talk*? There's something I'm simply bursting to ask?" at once she had left whatever she was doing (people, I must say, from top to bottom seemed to have quantities of time to devote to one) as if, like Liesl, she had been hoping that the American would again turn up.

It wasn't the most suitable spot in the world for this kind of talk. But another of the things learned, and learned fast, was to pitch in anywhere and dispense with preliminaries; and if it became necessary to shout a bit, or take on rather more than might have been bargained for (since bystanders

were apt, out of sheer proximity, to sidle into a discussion),
then that was the way it had to be done. Nobody was going
to say, "Let's step into the conservatory." And as a matter
of fact, the very awkwardness of the circumstances served, I
suppose, to precipitate intimacy. One could hardly, in this
space, minuet around a point. One learned, indeed — at a
crowded street corner, or eating in the congestion of a H-O
restaurant, or jammed against shirts in an S-Bahn car — to
ask the sort of questions that are as a rule launched quietly
and delicately, in an hour of rapprochement, by fading fire-
light or under first stars. These were, in brief, to be days
without small talk. Although the weather, for the most part,
was to remain superb, I can't remember even a "social" reference to the weather.

And so here one sat, on a bench against a wall, with the
hubbub of the Presse room occupying the air; one sat beside
a dark young woman named Käthe, who had a face with much
strength in it, and who was speaking English as if over crumpets in a Bloomsbury teashop.

I said this to her, and we both laughed.

"If you were in London in 1938, so was I. We might —
isn't it interesting? — have met each other."

"But isn't it much more interesting like this? To meet here,
in Alexanderplatz."

Admittedly it was! "But Käthe, why? Why on earth did
you come — to this side, I mean?"

"It seems so strange to you?"

"It seems downright idiotic! But you must have your
reasons. Especially since you brought your own children
back."

She told me why; and watching her, as she talked, I thought
how different from the tremulous and insecure lyricism of a

Liesl. For here was something hardy, integrated, compact: not, one felt, an arrangement of arguments but an organic position very far from negligible. It was an impression (to be received from Ernst as well) of a state of mentality without the gaps and blurrings — or the intuitive breakthroughs — which one accepts as normal in an exploratory human being. It was like the difference between a garden, subject to the hazards and miracles of growth, and a laboratory with shelves of bottled essences. And one felt as time and again one was to feel how untidy the first, how orderly the second! how *fruitful* on the one hand, and how *explosive* on the other.

Käthe spoke straightforwardly. At seventeen, it appeared, she had in some way been enabled to get to England, after both her parents had perished at Ausschwitz. Apparently they had been militant "enemies of the Reich"; and she spoke of them not as a daughter of parents but as one comrade speaks with respect of others. In London she had lived with an English family (the husband and her father had been student friends at Göttingen) and there she had married a year or two afterwards a young Polish Jew, himself later killed while serving with the British. The house in Hampstead had been twice bombed. Before she was twenty she had known what it was like to be a fugitive, an exile, and under attack. And at the end of the war she had returned to Germany.

"You wished to, Käthe? You chose to do so?"

"It is the country that murdered both my parents; it destroyed by the million my husband's people. I wanted to be of help — so that such things shouldn't ever again happen. The Gorhams understood. They too believed that Germany must be saved — must be changed — by the Germans themselves. So I returned to Stuttgart, because that is where my mother's relatives live; and I sent for my children the next

year because I wanted them to be a part of the new world we
must build. I wanted them to understand — as soon as they
could understand anything at all — how hard they must work,
to make that world." She had started in Stuttgart; then come
to Berlin. In less than twelve months she had deliberately,
decisively, of her own free will, crossed the line from West
to East.

"Because," she said, "I soon saw how it was. In the West
nothing really was going to be changed. Soon it would all be
the same again — the greed and deceit and every man for himself. The same old deals and investments," she said, "like a
great spiderweb. The same old world — patched up, not
changed! I saw people starving, and other people beginning
to be rich again. There were things in shops that nobody
had — but somebody bought them! somebody was already
coming out on top! The Germans can be very clever, you
know, if they're working for themselves — or think they are.
They can be twice as industrious as anybody else. And the
Americans — "

"Yes, Käthe? Fire away!"

For she had hesitated for a moment.

"I watched them," she said. "I watched the Americans,
and I saw how incredibly stupid they were being — if they
wanted a change; and how clever — if they *didn't!*"

And then, abruptly, it was she who was asking me a question; and asking it in such a way, on such a note of urgency,
that one realized she had been waiting from the first to voice
it.

"Why have people in the West so changed? People who
used to understand!"

"What people, Käthe? Who understand what?"

"The danger — the things they were fighting against!" she

said. "During the war we were all together, we were true comrades. Everybody saw what Fascism meant! Why have they changed?"

On a sudden impulse I asked, "People like the Gorhams?"

It could be seen in her face — the Gorhams above all!

And somehow it didn't seem difficult to understand. The personal experiencing of the Nazi horror; then the English family, liberal, or radical, with its Continental contacts (perhaps among the first to "recognize" Fascism); the young Pole — in revolt against a feudal past? and the wartime admiration of a besieged people for an heroic "ally." The "atmosphere" that had prevailed at the close of the war: Mr. Gromyko saying at San Francisco, "Try the red caviar!" — Natalia Sergeyeva inviting one to Moscow. One enemy still too raw in the mind for another to have succeeded it. The tide of events had hurtled a world forward; but Käthe still stood at that same point.

"I don't understand what has happened to them!" she said. "They were so fine, so intelligent! They were *good*," she said. "How can such people have turned against us?"

For a moment it might have been Liesl speaking. And one thought, "How remarkable a thing is love!" Six years of blinding distortions and lies, and still she must speak of the goodness she had known; as Ernst, later, was to say of Hank, "He is my friend."

"Käthe, it doesn't seem strange to me. It makes complete sense. Many things have happened since you came over here; and people who once believed as you do have had to face up to the hard facts. It hasn't been easy for them. I don't suppose the Gorhams changed overnight; but at some point they had to. I can quite understand."

"But at what point? What happened to make them do it?"

"Perhaps it was Czechoslovakia," I said. "I know two people who hung on until then, hoping like mad they'd be able to stick. But they simply couldn't stomach Czechoslovakia."

She said, sounding intent, "What do you mean?"

"Oh, Käthe, *really!* The Nazis took over other countries! What on earth have the Russians been up to in Europe?"

It was as if one had placed a textbook in her hand. "But that's preposterous! The Nazis conquered and destroyed other countries! Russia *protects!*" And sharply, impatiently, as if dealing out facts so elementary that it was almost a nuisance to take time off for them, she said, "Russia is threatened by the whole capitalist world; everyone knows that. She must protect herself — she'd be a fool if she didn't! — and in doing so she's protecting everything we stand for. Do you think we don't know what's happening across the border? The rest of Europe mobilized against us! The people of Germany, with a gun at their backs, being forced to re-arm — *forced* to!" she said. "The same German people we fought to *dis*-arm! Even the police — what are called the police! — wearing military helmets; drilling like soldiers! Do you think we don't know!"

And she asked then, "Would you rather have seen happen in Czechoslovakia what happened in *Spain?*"

"You're asking me," I reminded her, "why people changed. And I'm telling you why. If it sounds loony to you, I'm sorry, it's a pity; but it won't, of course, alter the fact. Because they *have* — and I'm not speaking, either, about reactionaries, or people who're politically illiterate to begin; but intelligent ones, informed one, like your own friends, Käthe. The sort of people who are as dead against Fascism today as they ever were. And blaze away, let me tell you, whenever it seems to them we're slipping from our principles — dickering with Spain, or bolstering up outworn elements anywhere. I bet anything the Gorhams haven't changed in that! Do you hear from them, incidentally?"

She didn't at once respond to the question; then, "They send the children presents at Christmas," she said; and, after that, "On their birthdays they write to them — " Why she went on I don't know; but she added, as if momentarily we were somewhere else. "They had a little dog — Lucy Locket." (And London it might have been, over crumpets, in a tea-shop.) "Lucy writes the letters. It's very English!" she said.

Then we were back in East Berlin, with the loudspeaker charging the air outside, and the posters of a taloned Uncle Sam, and bright-wreathed children, and "Friendship Wins!" She was saying, "They used to know how to decide — between truth and lies. Now they believe everything said against us. *People like that* — I can't understand it! Believing what they're told, just as the Germans did when told by Hitler!"

"Oh, come now, Käthe! With a bit of a difference! The Gorhams, after all, are getting both sides. You've lived in London, you know how it is — how anybody there can perfectly well listen to both Churchill *and* the Dean of Canterbury; and read both the *Times* and the *Daily Worker;* and stand up in Hyde Park and sound off about anything under the sun. Last month when I was there I heard a man accusing the American Government of deliberately starting the Korean war. Nobody interfered with him. He talked away to his heart's content. You could stand up yourself — saying exactly what you're saying to me now."

Very nearly, one felt, she asked what one expected her to: "One *still* can?" But the words were held back; and so I asked, instead, "I wonder what would happen if I went out

there — into Alexanderplatz — and started making a speech
about warmonger Stalin and the enslavement of people behind the Iron Curtain?"

"You would be stopped," she said, "because it is a lie." And
she said then, with a curious kind of intensity, as if passing
from an official to a personal statement, "Germany isn't England. You know that. If we had a Hyde Park here in Berlin,
people wouldn't laugh, the way the English do — " And she
said, as if throwing away minor points (rather as one was prepared to do oneself!) in an effort to communicate an essential
faith, "People aren't — don't you see! — to be trusted yet.
They must be schooled, like children who've never been
taught, or have been taught all wrong and must start again.
That is why it isn't an easy thing! We must root out evils
that are old and deep; we're changing a world — how could it
be easy!" And she asked, then, "Do you think I'd be here if
I didn't believe that! I could be in the West — with the
cream cakes and the automobiles and the night clubs and all
the rest of it. There's nothing to stop me. I could go now.
But I stay, because of what must be built. And it's hard, yes
— you can see for yourself how many things we must do without. And people must suffer, if they're stupid, or selfish, or
working against us. I know that too, and I wish it could be
different. But every creative thing in life is painful — as
having a child is painful. And it's better to be a part of a hard
birth than of something soft and easy and dead!"

And gradually, as she talked, one received a single and overwhelming impression. It was as if she were speaking from a
pulpit, not a platform: delivering, instead of a political dia-
tribe, a religious pronouncement; a stern sermon. It was an
impression one was to receive from Ernst as well. A kind of
puritanism: not to be misconstrued or disparaged — or so

done to our own high cost. For to pose against it, to dangle cheerfully and confidently like a carrot, the "superior advantages" offered by the West, was, one saw, to miscalculate the very instinct basically involved. It was to do what we are all too prone to do — with our faith not only in the happy ending but our tendency to settle, before the ending's reached, for approximate happinesses: the unexacting, the mediocre, the immature thing. It was, one saw, to underestimate *the idealist's capacity for sacrifice.*

To a Käthe, the "easy" was equated with the "decadent"; the "material" assets with a "moral" deficiency. Not only was deprivation a conceded fact, it was a banner flown: the very proof in a way of the fortitude evoked by the "magnitude" of a cause. (Later Ernst was to take me to a film, and there was the thesis, unflinchingly set forth: the heroine in shirt sleeves, a straightforward girl; the hero "seduced" in West Berlin by a sexy charmer, Hollywood style, with her furs and jewels and cocktails and guile; the "people's" cause, the conspiratorial clique; the rigors of the right and the allurements of the wrong!) There was even, it seemed to one, in this hallowing of hardship, a good part of the reason for Käthe's undismissable admiration of the English. She had seen them under fire; they had grit and stamina and loyalty, and didn't whine. The Spartan virtues. The virtues she herself had early received as so high a heritage. Her parents had died for what they believed; and there was that in their daughter which directly sought — which even demanded of life, one felt, in a way both frightening and potentially magnificent — totality of cause and the act of total dedication to it.

One might have been listening to a young priestess, committed sacrificially to a religious order. And one thought (it was sharply to be thought many times): against this we can pitch no lesser faith! no easy assumptions, no stereotyped creed. One thought of all the people who risk nothing in life; who offend at no point because at no point offensive — who keep silent when to speak is a hazardous act, or say the convenient, the uncostly thing. All the people who play safe; get by; never err. The cautious, the respectable, the *below* reproach, because never emerging into embattled airs; never penalized for a conviction during their lives and never, afterwards, saluted for it. For one thought, too, of the way the world moves — of the stupendous forward thrust of events and how it has been from time immemorial impulsed, not by circumspect men, but by prophets and heroes and poets and rebels: by those in whom flamed some vision or concern forever, as it appears, the suspect thing, and always, when accepted, the new status quo.

Those who act in the world, risking failure and mistake; and those who, doing nothing, are exempt from blame.

One thought of them, sitting here on a bench and listening. And it seemed an irony of the first order that this girl, Käthe, at some point in herself (call it what one chose; and tragically perverted though the expression of it had become) — at some point should be allied to the positive, not the negative: to the movers of the earth, and not the withholders. There was, one saw, some instinct here not to be discredited; not to be destroyed. For to stamp out a flame is to create ash, not light. And too much of our world has been brought to ashes: to disillusionment, cynicism, bitterness, contempt. If, in defeating the falsity of a doctrine, we defeat, too, the capacity to believe — how sorry the outcome; what a shadowy company of those who are left only *against*, not *for*: with the will to hate, without the heart to love.

Suddenly I wanted to see it saved, this impulse in Käthe,

or whatever one called it; suddenly it seemed of the utmost value. I don't know if what I said was the right thing to say; but I found myself, faced by her own intensity, wanting to stand clear of the easy "advantages," of the prosperity and pleasures and indulgences of a world: I wanted to be in shirt sleeves too! in my own way, and for a truer reason.

"Käthe, I believe you mean what you say. I believe you care, with your whole heart. And I honor that caring — I want you to know that, because there's where we can meet; where we are meeting! But the way you've chosen — that's something else. That seems to me, I'm afraid, fantastically wrong, because I can't, like you, draw such a line between ends and means. If you're persuaded it's really so — that tyranny can somehow mature a people, that hate breeds fellowship — then that's your business. That's what you must act on; I can quite see that. But I wish we had you on *our* side! We could do with you, Käthe! — not your *opinions*, which I utterly reject, but you yourself. Your fortitude, and your selflessness. Because if you think everything in the West is a picnic, then you just ought to try it. You just ought to see! It's tough going, believe me — not in the way it is over here, but at another level, more exactingly, I think; at least if one happens to believe, as you do, that a new world is being born. Because that we can agree about; I believe it too. It seems as inevitable as light, doesn't it? Something is happening, humanity-wide — and there's no stopping it, no going back. But I believe, Käthe, a thousand times over, that it must come from us, from our way of doing things — the way of Hyde Park, if you want to put it like that — if only we can stick to our own highest principles, and see the implications of them intelligently enough. We make all sorts of wretched mistakes, and fall into betrayals that are pretty sickening. And

we get scared — which is bad business; and because we're
scared, start mistrusting one another. For there are those in
the West — not many of them, but they're noisy! — who
interestingly enough believe what you yourself have just said.
That other people aren't *to be trusted to decide.* You believe
that, I know, because of your particular feeling about the Germans; but they say the same thing about their fellow Americans. Everybody, they believe — which always means everybody else, doesn't it? — should be allowed to know only what
it's *safe* for him to know. The orthodox thing; the uncon-
troversial. For instance, instead of *answering* Karl Marx,
they'd stuff him into a closet — as if there weren't any answer.
Perhaps, at bottom, that's what they're scared of! Perhaps, I
mean, it's not people they distrust, but truth itself. It could
be that, couldn't it? For why, otherwise, should they presume
to 'protect' us by using the very methods of the system we're
against?"

And one said, risking it, "As a matter of fact, it may well
be that for the next stretch of time we're going to have to face,
and individually think out, something pretty serious. Domestically, I mean — in America itself, involving our relations
with one another. Because fear, I suppose, is something new
to us; it's taken us unawares, and we've been sent into a spin
by it — with those who are unscrupulously shaping it to their
own ends still not clearly enough recognized by everybody.
Fortunately we're safe from what you tragically know yourself
— the liquidation of opponents. But it's grave, just the same,
this distrust among ourselves, and we're going to have to learn,
and learn fast, how to deal with it like responsible and honor-
able citizens. And besides all this, which is a crisis development — what quantities of other wrong things there are!
Vulgar and slovenly and humiliating things, that could make

one at times almost tear one's hair out. Do you know, for instance, that, as a nation, we spend in a year seven — or is it ten — times as much of our income on liquor and films as we do on *education?* Isn't that a fine feather in anybody's cap! How the Russian statistics could flatten us out there! And our race relations, look at them too — " For since this issue was bound to arise, it seemed only sensible to introduce it oneself. "They aren't, naturally, one tenth — one twentieth! — as grisly as they're made out to be over here; but so long as there's any problem at all, obviously it will remain our Achilles' heel. Because we can't get away from our own stated premise. Either it's true, or it's a sentimental myth. And the reassuring thing — if one happens to be particularly concerned about this; and I am; I have Negro friends — is the fact that the problem's now out in the open, and being seen in its relationship to a whole world. In a way, of course, we can thank you for this! I mean, the propaganda attacks against us have shown that until we practice what we preach we're bound to provide a target for attack. We can even, it seems to me, be grateful for this! At any rate it guarantees that we'll have to keep going, since one can hardly loll back, or settle for subterfuges, with half a world hotly breathing down one's neck."

This was, of course, in literally every conversation one had, to prove the trickiest issue of them all. For here was the ground upon which the opposition (however shaky in other respects) felt itself to stand with full, incontestable moral superiority. So unfailingly was this the case, and so equipped could people be with undeniable facts — as well as with the outrageous fallacies to be expected — that in the end one would have liked to propose to Congress a bill providing free passage to Berlin for every bigot and hoodlum in the United States, every irresponsible official and citizen: so they could hear and see for themselves what devastating damage they were personally doing to the America in whose name they presumed to act.

This one could even say to Käthe. And say, after it, "Don't you see what I mean by its not being easy? With all these factors and elements to be dealt with. But what I believe — and the Gorhams, I suppose, must believe it too — is that however faulty the process, however dishearteningly clumsy and slow, it's still for us the only possible way. We can see no intelligent, no decent alternative. Just as for you, in 1938, the British Government — deplorably muddled though it was — must have seemed an incomparably superior thing to Hitler's Reich. And incomparably, Käthe, is what I mean! Beyond compare! To think for oneself; to decide; to act — to move under law, by free choice, and in the open — it's the course we'll stick to, you can depend upon that. And what I can't help wondering, if it's hardship we're talking about, is if yours isn't really the easier way. For surely it's easier, when one comes right down to it, to do without the cream cakes and the nylons and so on than to undertake to think things through for oneself. Isn't that, after all, the toughest of jobs? And the reason why so few of us are found really doing it?"

At the end one nearly said something else.

It was something one was to feel a number of times — not with everyone, of course, and never again, perhaps, as sharply, as incisively as one felt it now. It was a conviction so suddenly and clearly *there*, that one very nearly said, "Oh, Käthe, when it happens, do get in touch with me! Do let me know, right away!" For this myth she had embraced was going to fail her. That was the assurance; here at the end. At some point, and in terms that she as an individual wouldn't any longer be able to rationalize, the falsity was going to disclose itself. *To* her, *Käthe* — specifically and inescapably. Because there existed in her this authentic concern (or whatever the verity was that one felt); because of the very nature and necessity of a lie which, when pressed, has only one course: to ruinously intensify and extend itself. At some point, straight ahead, this would come to pass.

One didn't know then, on that summer afternoon, the turn of events already being shaped. One wouldn't, I suppose, have even hazarded a guess as to what sort of challenge would eventually confront Käthe: what form it would take, what precise terms. The fact that her father and husband had been Jews didn't cross one's mind in any pointed way — not in that Festival dramatization of the racelessness of a cause, that pounding insistence upon a "world crusade" driving through all national and ethnic frontiers. It was obvious enough that the *sentiment* in evidence didn't constitute the *strategy*: it was the strategy evoking and manipulating the sentiment. But one had seen for oneself the assembled peoples, the yellow and white and black all mixed; one had heard the great cry of "Freundschaft!" go up, and the voices intermingled in the same song — even experiencing, as an individual American (surrounded by the signs saying "Ami Go Home!"), a degree of hospitality that couldn't be denied; so that one would have said that this particular fact — this calculated and brilliant exploitation of the "universal" — was not only intrinsic but in hard-cash terms, downright indispensable to the over-all campaign. If anyone had announced that in another six months the Kremlin would begin issuing, to internal security officials, confidential requests for incriminating data on prominent members of Jewish communities — if anyone at that particular point had announced such a thing, it would, I suppose, have sounded, not ethically implausible, heaven knows, but strategically improbable. So there was nothing to go on that afternoon. Or nothing that I had the prescience to detect. There was simply the spontaneous, the overwhelming conviction that in due time, and with inexorable logic, something spurious would *betray itself* to this girl.

Such a conviction — obviously enough! — could be converted into an all too balmy doctrine. Let evil ride its course and eventually it will fail. (As perhaps, who knows, eventually it might: if what it opposed were sufficiently without flaw — offering nothing for it to batten upon!) But the picture could hardly be simplified to that! For there weren't only the Käthes, the Liesls, the Ernsts: those with whom one was to experience this outleap of expectancy; there was the baby too, in Alexanderplatz — the small fist guided into a greeting to Moscow; there were the blue-eyed little girls with their Mädchen braids, and the little boys with grubby knees and caps clapped on anyhow. There were the thousands, the millions growing up in these airs. Day by day being shaped to a course. One could hardly fall back, in the face of such a world, upon the comforting "inevitability" of a process. For the process wasn't an abstraction in space. Not a diagram on a page, or a newspaper headline. It was children, and men and women, and boys and girls, and the hearts of them, the minds, the very tissue of being; and to say "in due time," or "let evil take its course," was to speak of *them*, not of formulas or equations; for an hour or a year wasn't a calendar on a wall or a clock ticking but lives being lived, and seed, and growth, and the surge of beliefs that precede events. . . .

There was no balmy doctrine to relax on here!

Nevertheless, here it was, this particular assurance. (And an assurance, in Käthe's case, that was to prove correct.) The job on our own side was hammered plain: to outproduce, out-mobilize, outmaneuver, outmatch; but wasn't there, too, at another level, a way in which — by faith — we must out-endure?

Now we were standing again, and shaking hands; and I wondered for a moment if something had been lost. We had sat down so easily, so eager to talk; where were we now in relation to each other?

"I've appreciated it, Käthe — your talking with me like this."

She didn't answer for a moment; then, "If you have time, perhaps you would come and see me?"

"Oh, yes! I'd love to."

"To my home, I mean."

"And meet the children?"

"Yes, I would like you to meet my children." And she said, after that, "I'll make us all an English cup of tea!"

Later I was to send to Käthe something written that day, in 1939, when a voice from the London she was then a part of had momentously announced, "Since nine o'clock this morning a state of war has existed — "

> Walking in a quiet way
> I heard today
> an old man say:
> "Would you rather see your foe
> driven low
> or driven high?
> Reply!
> Reply!
> Would you rather see your foe
> suffer harm
> or suffer change?
> On a point as needle-small
> trembles all."

It was strange
walking in so still a way,
in a twilight of alarm,
this to hear an old man say.

VII

On that first afternoon spent with Ernst we walked simply miles in the brilliant summer sun.

He said at once, when we met, "You haven't worn more shoes!" (I had on, as before, rather fragmentary sandals.) "Oh, I'll manage," I said. "We aren't much given to boots, you know — or iron heels!" He laughed; and said, "Now I'll show you Berlin." And I thanked my stars that although I'm a pitiful specimen at games I can walk, practically forever, and keep up with the sort of stride these Germans are good at.

To begin with, we went foraging for the blue shirt.

These, it appeared, were issued only at certain points: small, strictly utilitarian shops — dense with a kind of dun-serge-gloom — which seemed, atmospherically, less allied to commerce than to officialdom itself, as if the merchandise had been prescribed by a Central Committee and produced from blueprints rather than patterns. There were shelves piled solid with serviceable stuffs. There would, one felt, be nothing to waver between: if an article were needed, here it would be. Not innumerable versions of it, some better, some worse; but a basic "it." And one thought suddenly: for three fourths of the world this is the need! A coat on the back; bread in the mouth. And one thought too (as if it were something on another planet) of Bonwit Teller on Fifth Avenue; of the thousand glittering and frivolous elegancies; of the etceteras we can afford — not only to buy, but to conceive of, to devise, to give brain and hand to. "Shall I have the jeweled lizard or the sequined scarf?" How extraordinary! that one should ever have weighed such things! That such exquisite trivia should exist at all! It wasn't that the etceteras seemed suddenly "wrong" — after a fashion they could be rated as a kind of minor poetry: little triolets, little epigrams wrought out of rhinestone and feathers and tulle. It was just that all at once they seemed worlds away; a meaningless glitter on another planet.

One very soon found that Ernst, as an escort, was singularly effective. Without palaver, and without noticeably exhibiting credentials, he commanded everywhere immediate attention — although he couldn't, as a matter of fact, evoke a shirt. For we were told at each of the shops the same thing: they were clean sold out of them, and no wonder indeed! considering the floods of blue in the streets. So he bought instead one of the little caps banded with flags ("The American flag as well," he pointed out) and, after that, in what appeared to be the official issuing place for them, a dove-of-peace stickpin which, when stuck on me, almost at once lost its head. "I suppose," I said, "the shock's too much for it!" And he said, "Some of our workmanship is poor. It is still hard for us, with so much to do."

I had asked at the outset about the posters: would it be possible to get any of the smaller ones — "To take back with me to America; they'd be interested in seeing them." So we headed next through streets less crowded and pleasantly leafed to the building from which the posters were being distributed. Here everybody shook hands and said "Freundschaft!" cordi-

ally; and although it was German posters I asked for, they insisted, with a courtesy that remained adamantine, upon my
having English ones — or the ones, that is, that were cap-
tioned in English: rather as Liesl had tried with the same
eagerness to steer the Frenchmen to the French interpreter.
But see! all of you have been especially provided for! — there
was something a little touching in the insistence on this. As
if it were an inclusiveness so unique, so unprecedented, that
it was bound to stagger the honest guest! The posters brought
out were the decorative ones, naturally: the garlanded children, interracially linked, and a bright blue panel with
"Friendship" handsomely lettered on it in gold; and pressed
upon me, as an added treat, were the enormous faces one
couldn't get away from: Stalin and Grotewohl and President
Pieck, each of them so massively, so inexorably avuncular,
exuding such wisdom, strength and kindliness that they might,
like Good Shepherds, have graced a nursery.

"Your leaders have such *big* faces!" I said.

And Ernst said, "Our leaders are big men."

Outside again, on the next trek, we stopped at a street
corner beside a stall to drink from bottles a pinkish Limonade
(lukewarm and rather horrid, with a flavor I could relate to
nothing hitherto known); and at once several shabbily dressed
women gathered around, with small children at their heels,
and two or three of those endearing little German dogs which
aren't dachshunds but palpably at some point in their ancestry have been intimately associated with one, so that a
familiar terrier head can unconcernedly top off four inchling
legs. "American? English?" the women wanted to know.
"American," Ernst told them — with that just perceptible
note of proprietorship; only coming into play when we were
involved with other people. And out came the handgrips and

the slogan-greetings, accompanied this time by a more feminine interest. For they were, one realized, fascinated by the
patchwork cotton skirt. I turned it up a bit, showing them
how Peck and Peck had fashioned it, since it occurred to me
that they might make use of the idea. "You could cut up any
old things of your own, in different shapes — see? It's quite
simple." "Ah, schön! schön! — " they were charmed with
the ingenuity. And one of them, a ruddy and strapping soul,
obviously under the impression that I'd dreamed forth and
executed the style myself, gave me a thumping congratulatory
whack. There was something warming and domestic about it
all! What simplicities there were, underneath the divisions;
what commonplace sharings. One wondered for a moment if
the Voice of America mightn't, on the side, take to this sort
of thing. "Here's a new way, Frauen, to serve your stale
Pumpernickel — " or "Have you tried this: for deodorizing
sauerkraut, or making lamp bases from beer bottles, or dyeing
that outfit you're sick and tired of — "

Now one of the little dogs (pitched between puppyhood
and the next stage) who had hurled himself forward, all agog,
tried to lift a leg against Ernst's trouser; tottered; tumbled;
and resorted, looking crestfallen, to a baby squat. And all of
us, as we stood there, burst out laughing. Anywhere in the
world we could have laughed! The strapping woman, as if
thinking the words herself, said, "It is the same in America,
yes!" "The same!" I said. And now a child on the outskirts,
a little girl of perhaps five, with the air of one pining to be included in the festivities, suddenly presented something, shoot-
ing it out at arm's length. It was a button, with a dove on it;
and it felt warm and sticky, as if she'd been holding it, a prized
possession, tight and safe in a hot hand. I thought she was
simply showing it to me; but apparently it was a gift; I was

supposed to keep it. "Freundschaft!" she said, beaming up. A rather plain little girl, with a runny nose, who looked as if prize possessions occurred rarely. I gave her, in return, the comb from my bag. There was nothing else to give — for one came (as one was advised to) deliberately unencumbered on these expeditions, carrying only the official Festival pass and one's military orders. "An *American* comb!" I said, although combs, one realized, were among the articles and functions a trifle difficult to nationalize! The little girl, however, appeared no end pleased. When we went on again, leaving them behind, she and the other children, in a small absorbed group, were taking turns in combing one another's hair.

It was after this that gradually I became aware of something. We were still on streets that were relatively quiet (away, at any rate, from the central hullaballoo) and the company I was in, it now became evident, wasn't recommending me to everyone encountered. There were older people who, after a curious glance, looked aside. They were going about their business, drably dressed; not celebrating "peace" or "brotherhood" or anything; with a set, sticking-it-out air to them; dispirited, taciturn — that was how they seemed: an impression that was to gather in the time ahead precision and force. A sense of waiting, without expectancy; of dulled endurance, rather than resistance. People who weren't starving or enraged or in despair; not existing melodramatically in a state of terror, but going about their business, day in, day out, keeping their mouths shut, closing their doors. One was to have the feeling that if one walked on, on and on through the forbidden Zone, there would be millions upon millions of people like this.

I said to Ernst, "How *sad* many seem!" And he said back quickly, "Only the old ones! They have no hope — that's why they aren't of any use to us today. The youth believes! It's the youth that works!"

A theme to be reiterated time and again. The older people were no longer to be turned to or depended upon; they were tired, or fixed in an outworn mold; without courage, or vision, or the will to aspire. Nobody was to speak of them as if they constituted an "opposition"; they were a passive, a negligible element, it seemed — discounted as participants in the task at hand with a kind of pity, even with a measure of sympathetic understanding. "They were never taught what we've learned to do — to work together; for themselves, yes, but not for something bigger than themselves." "Didn't they work for Fascism, Ernst?" "Fascism," he said, "*was* themselves."

There was the passivity, the resignation, true enough, in many of the faces seen on the streets. But not only, one was to find, among the older people; and not always, either, in the same kind of terms.

For there were those encountered when I was by myself: waiting for Ernst at a restaurant table, or traveling back and forth on the S-Bahn trains. There were the three boys met with that same evening (one beside me and two on the seat opposite) who, at the last station on the Russian side — as the Eastern police came through the car and all the blue-shirted youths surged out on to the platform — just perceptibly stiffened, their eyes blank. When the train, nearly emptied, went on aagin, I said in English, "Good! you made it." They laughed; and the oldest of them (he was nineteen, one learned) said, "Oh, it's easy! We've been over three times." I asked how they happened to have ordinary clothes. "We hear that your things are held by group leaders, and only given back to you the day you leave." He shrugged, and said lightly, "Everything's not to be believed in the world!" He had a cool, uninvolved, ironic air; there was a kind of deftness to him, both physically and mentally, so that one felt he would be nimble in a pinch, not easily caught out because at no point committed. When I enquired about "conditions" in the Soviet Zone — two of them came from Jena and the third from Dresden — he said, "Oh, it's not as bad as the West says." "You aren't coming over then, seriously, to stay?" "Why should I?" he asked. "Unless you can prove you're a political refugee, there's no work for you; you're no better off." And he said in that light and skimming way, "I've a job; I've a girl. Life goes on!" When I asked in what direction he expected it to go on, he said, "People in the East all want the same thing. No more war, and to be left alone." "Left alone by whom?" "By everybody," he said. "Russians, Americans, British — everybody!" I spoke of the Festival, and he dismissed it with a phrase: a "big show," foisted upon them. He himself had had to work twelve hours a day, for the two weeks previous to his arrival in Berlin. "Everybody had to; to make up the time they'll be away." One of the others volunteered the information that many of the boys and girls were "very tired" — "They sleep all the time; they don't want to march." And the oldest one asked, "How many do you think would come if they didn't have to?" "I've no idea. How many would?" He shrugged again, as if it weren't worth answering; but the third boy, the youngest (not more than fourteen or fifteen, one judged), said, "I'd come — just to see!" "I think," I told him, "that I would too." And because he looked ready for any diversion, I asked if he'd heard about the public discussions that the American State Department was at the moment conducting. "They're open to anyone, and anything can be talked about — that's what they're for, to answer questions." The oldest

boy laughed. "Questions!" he said. "But we know the answers. We know what they'll say! Russia's all bad — America's all good!" And he said then, "And what difference does
it make? Everything will go on just the same!"

He was only nineteen; but he had a certain kind of knowledge. The knowledge, cool and clinical in his head, that
under any regime on earth life can be lived between the lines:
noncommittally, inconspicuously, without allegiance or revolt. Life can "go on," with a job, a girl — and, if it stops, a
bullet is a bullet on either side, and you're as dead in the
West as you are in the East.

"Over there," Ernst was saying, as we strode along, "what
are they governed by? The old men of Bonn! Here you can
see for yourself how it is. The youth must accept the responsibility. The work is ours; and we know what depends upon
us!"

"And what does, Ernst? What depends upon you?"

"The peace of the world and the unity of our country."

A tall order! But it had to be tall. That was the point; that
was the spell.

"And all the youth here — they all think that?"

"You saw them yesterday. You saw what they mean."

"But what about those who are clearing out? They're coming over in droves; we see that too."

He said, with severity, with a kind of scorn, "There are
those in any country who think only of themselves. If that's
what they are, it is good they go! The West is welcome to
them!"

I was to think of both that and the boy on the S-Bahn —
standing in the bunker to which Regina was to take me.

The corridors weren't wide enough for two to walk abreast,

and in the doorways of the concrete cell-like rooms, lit by naked electric bulbs, crowded three, four, even five people: watching us, grasping our hands when we paused, each seeking to communicate in the few minutes we were allowed not the urgency and complexity of a collective problem, but his own difficulties, his own peculiar hardships and plight. Only by special permission could one be here. (Journalists were anathema to those in charge! — since the last one, admitted several months before, had used names and facts in a sensationalized story that had precipitated reprisals against a family left behind.) All questioning was supervised by the official assigned to us, and one kept stopping short, feeling clumsy, inexpert, as if moving among spidery ambiguities and uncertainties. For this was one of the receiving points, this huge bunker, deep underground, where those coming over from the Russian Zone — without explicit proof of being political refugees — were sheltered and held for rigorous screening. Here were farmers and professors and mechanics and clerks; young couples, and whole families with small children or aged grandparents: some freshly arrived and some marooned here, one found, for weeks on end, even for months — human beings with names one was forbidden to ask; without even the solace of normal camaraderie, for officially they were discouraged from too intimately mingling (cheek by jowl though the horde of them must exist) since no one could be sure of the role of another and over all must hang that reprisal-fear since each had left behind something of his life.

Up and down corridor after corridor we were to go; past cell after cell, group after group — with the faces turned to us holding, it seemed, all the moods and motives common to humanity. Faces strained and eager and exhausted and glum; inward faces, composed or wan, and those with a look so flatly

normal as to appear, here, almost indecent — a mother cheerfully mending a child's sock, a boy reading a paper-backed
novel to a girl; bold faces and apathetic ones and plaintive and
shrewd; and still others in which one seemed to detect a
panic-regret for a rash move. If it was heroes one had expected and heroines, they weren't here — or not recognizably
so. Nothing notable or stirring or selfless was being said; on
the contrary, many sounded bewildered or distraught, even
bitter with their demands that something "be done." "Why
are we held in such a place? Why aren't we permitted — or
given — or sent — " Each was identified with his own pre-
dicament, with the knowledge that a step so drastic had been
taken that everything familiar was irrevocably forfeited with
nothing else yet to hold to in its stead. And suddenly, listening to them, one was sharply to think: *But where are the
Ernsts?* Who among these was prepared to say, "First, world
peace; second, a united Germany; third, myself"? Why had
they come over here at all? — for how cloudy and equivocal
motives appeared: to better one's own prospects, to escape an
accusation; because a job was lost, or something wasn't liked,
or somebody else was heading across, and so why not too with
so little to lose? "The West is welcome to them!" Ernst had
said. And one was suddenly to ask: what are they bringing?
what are they *for*? Was this all we had to pose against the
other: people running away — against people who "believed"?
It was necessary to assume, it was a cardinal assumption of
this rigidly drawn hour, that anyone who "chose freedom" was
morally superior to anyone found standing on the other side.
But suddenly it didn't seem as simple as that. How did one
compare a dedicated Käthe, deliberately choosing to "do
without," with a man or woman querulously complaining,
"Why aren't we taken better care of when we come? Why

can't I go — or have — or be given — " Why? why? why?
they asked. Reaching out urgently and reiterating their woes.
Then we came to and stopped beside the young man.

For a moment, and superficially, he reminded me of Ernst:
there was the same height, the same ease of bearing, and they
were, one judged, more or less of an age, the late twenties or
early thirties. He had a keen look to him; his handclasp was
strong. He stood as if at the helm of a ship or on a mountain-
top in a race of wind; and, as he talked — he was a shoemaker,
and came from "a certain small village" — gaiety leaped un-
defeatably into his face. "We are sardines, yes? Just able to
wiggle! But we can always make room for you, if you'd care
to join us!" I asked how long he had been in this place; and
he said, "Five months." "Five months?" I repeated, thinking
I'd misheard. But five months it was, here like this: belonging
nowhere and acknowledged by no one. Suspended, one realized, or tried to realize, in a kind of hiatus, a state at the same
time blank as air and implacably barred. When I asked him
(for it was another of the brilliant afternoons) why at least
he wasn't out walking in the streets, he said simply, "I've
been walking for six hours; one can't, you know, walk all the
time." He spoke with courtesy, excusing my ignorance. He
stood there underground in a concrete cell, without any name
to him and from an unnamed place. He stood there with the
ranging look of an eagle; and I found myself suddenly, as if
delegated to do so, saying, "Thank you! Thank you for coming!" For there was no one else present, from any distance
away, to bid him welcome — to acknowledge what he was.
"We need good shoes!" "I make them!" he said. And one
thought: Chalk up one shoemaker to our side! Although
nothing had been declaimed for a Congressional Committee;
no fine protestations; no big words. He hadn't said, "At last

I'm a free man!" — which would have been nonsense; since he was no such thing; or rather, it would have misstated the truth, for the freedom that he had was a dimension of himself: it could neither be taken from him, nor bestowed, by the West. In "a certain small village" he had made his choice. He hadn't been cowed, or confused, or seduced. And he hadn't come over here for a softer thing. For there was that in his bearing, in the very mood and mettle of him, that matched what steeled a Käthe or an Ernst. He was the only one encountered there in the bunker of whom one was to feel precisely this. But such ones come singly, perhaps, and seldom; anywhere on earth. And because of this, all the others for some reason seemed suddenly more real: all these people herded together; for each of them, however imperfect his motivation, had at any rate taken this same step. At some point each one of them had come to a decision, clearly or cloudily, and had acted upon it — the wife abandoning her things-of-home (there was a flowered teapot on the shelf above her, "She wouldn't leave her teapot!" the husband said); the professor his library (three volumes he had brought); the young student his parents and a still younger brother ("I have come first, to find work; he will follow"). How easy to say the word "refugee." But what had gone into each of these moves? What intermeshed habits and loyalties and affections, to be torn apart like living tissue, and roots wrenched up, like roots from flesh? What last-minute waverings there must have been, with the hand on the door and the head turned — with the lamplight, irrecoverable if stepped from now, on the dishes, the books, the mother's face. . . .

Ordinary people, all lumped together. Not heroes and heroines; not valiant and invincible figures on posters, or statues of stone that never quake or slump. Just a mixture of

people, with not enough of them yet — not nearly enough —
standing as one shoemaker among them was to stand. But
people, nevertheless, who had made a move.

Walking through the streets of East Berlin, I asked Ernst
suddenly where he had picked up the English he spoke. For
one was struck again by the Midwest accent, so different from
the English of one's German friends who had been taught by
governesses or early in schools.

"I learned it from Hank."

"Who's Hank?" I asked.

"He's an American," he said.

I waited for more; but already one had found that he told
what he chose, and when he chose to tell it.

"Is he here — in Berlin?"

"No, he lives in Nebraska."

And he said, after that, "He was my friend."

We stopped off next, for twenty minutes or so — as one
might stop off in anybody's office while he checked on a call
or left a message — at, of all places, the Volkspolizei headquarters. Here Ernst excused himself in order to "attend" to
something (his manners were to remain throughout these
days a curious compound of the offhand and the punctilious)
while I waited for him on a bench in a large room. "She's
with me, a friend," he had briefly explained. And although
one hadn't exactly picked him, it was, by now, evident enough
that even if one had tried one could hardly have done better!
For apparently he exercised here too, within the fold as well
as without, a convenient amount of personal authority. The
police, of whom there were a considerable number, were, in
their attitude, both sociable and respectful. "Guten Tag,
Fräulein." "Guten Tag," one said, glad to sit down for a bit,

after the territory covered. Booted, and with guns stuck
blackly in their holsters, they were coming and going and conferring at desks; and it was all so easy and matter-of-fact that
several minutes elapsed before one thought, fully grasping it:
Well, really! fancy being *here* — feeling oneself suddenly back
at the beginning, at that initial encounter when, with Friedl,
there one had sat, hair on end, as the Russian stepped sharply
into the corridor of the train to call out the single word
"Police!" In the middle of nowhere and the depth of the
night, how alarming it had seemed! how enigmatic and sinister
the characters! And now — one casually sat like this! Right
here; in their own stronghold!

It was as if, one realized, a line had been drawn. Something
had strangely rounded itself off. The elderly woman, with her
umbrella and darned gloves, the children curled limp as kittens on the bench and Siegfried imperturbably paring a sausage — one was back at that point, in the darkness, in the cold,
with the guard pausing close to us to softly ask, "How is it,
how are things in the West?" and the girl turned warningly,
the air taut. In a way that couldn't in the least have been
planned, something had curved through space and time: from
there to here, from that to this.

And it struck one now, as one sat here watching them, how
ordinary all human beings could seem when, without fear,
they were squarely looked at. "Ordinary" perhaps wasn't quite
the word — but these young men, each with an individualized
face and voice, going about their business, some convivially,
some detached, how unsinister they appeared in the afternoon
sun! how unremarkable! Mightn't one indeed (if there
weren't on the walls any give-away posters, and the uniforms
were unknown and the language changed) mightn't one — in
all honesty — be almost anywhere? Could it really be said

that if one were dropped through a hole in the roof, with nothing to go on but the immediate impression, one instantly would exclaim, "Aha, the enemy!" Were they brutalized, these faces, or villainous, or degenerate? Did they literally show signs of a war-like urge? "Guten Tag, Fräulein." "Guten Tag," one returned. A number of rather shabbily uniformed young men, some of them looking one thing and some another: vigorous, lackadaisical, restive, slack — a cross-section of moods and temperaments and types, so that one could visualize them in a poolroom, or at a dance, or racing a motorcycle, or (since they were Germans) picking wildflowers somewhere on a day off. Later in the evening on Stalin Allee, when several truckloads of them were to pass us, all singing and waving, Ernst was to say, "There is what the West calls our army!" And one had to admit that by and large they didn't strike the eye as a martial lot. Except, of course, that they all carried guns.

And one would, suddenly, have liked to say aloud, "It's all very well, boys, Guten-Tag-ing me — but what's on the agenda, this fine summer day? What orders are being issued, from the top down?" Or to say, perhaps, "Do you know what? — once I was held up by some of you myself! With a gun pointed at me. A gun like your own."

Outside once more, as we again strode off, I did say this — on an impulse — to Ernst.

"What do you mean? Where were you held?"

"I was taken off a train, coming to Berlin. With a group of other people; eleven of us there were."

"Was anyone hurt?"

"No, no one was hurt."

"Why were you taken off?" he sharply asked.

"I didn't, I'm afraid, have the proper papers." For such, after all, had been the case.

He said, in that voice of impersonal severity, "The rules are given. They must be obeyed."

"Yes, I know. I only mentioned it because it's never actually happened to me before. A gun, I mean."

"Your films," he said, "are full of guns. It's all they do — shoot one another! We have nothing in Germany to compare with that!"

"Our films, Ernst, fortunately aren't us."

"Even your children play with such things. The toys of the West — we know what they are! Guns and tanks and fighter planes!"

One didn't have to cross into the East to hear this. Even Klaus had said, "There are things about America that frighten the European; you must understand that, or you will fail to credit us where we should be credited. We, too, can be *morally* disturbed!"

"Toys! — so they'll learn to make war," Ernst said, "even in their games! And the books they have, we've seen those too! People murdering one another, and women without clothes. Picture books sold to children!" he said; and he asked, "Do you think any German child is to be found with such things? Go anywhere — see for yourself!"

A usual answer was of course at hand. American children might have lethal playthings, and comic-strip violence to feed the mind on — but at any rate we'd yet to produce a generation of racial fanatics, or political imbeciles, capable of an Auschwitz or a mass Heil. An answer familiarly, and legitimately, resorted to. With history as witness. But there were times when suddenly the words got stuck; when they didn't seem good enough; or safe enough perhaps! — for could we be sure, facing the barbarisms in our own civilization, that the returns were all in yet: that there mightn't lie ahead a whirlwind it would be no fun to reap? The words suddenly could stick in the throat, and the stock argument, "If we are at fault, you're incomparably worse!" remain undelivered: answering no one because failing oneself. One thought of the German woman earlier encountered, in the West not the East, on the outskirts of Bonn, with a patch over an eye socket and one arm gone. (For along with the ruins in a country such as this are the number of human beings with bits of themselves missing.) She had been standing near a handsome requisitioned villa, where several little boys were playing gangsters. "Bang! bang! bang!" they had shouted at each other, pretending to fall dead with dramatic groans. She had stood there, the German woman, watching the Americans. There had been in her face something like hate.

Ernst, abruptly, as if an idea had just occurred to him, was changing our course in the middle of the street. "I'll show you what they have, our children," he said; and at the next U-Bahn entrance that we came to he hesitated momentarily, then swung inside.

"What!" I said. "You're letting me *ride!*"

And free too — for he strode past the ticket collector as if she didn't exist.

"You're a very convenient escort, Ernst! What exactly are you — anything I should know?"

And it was then that one learned his rank and role. Chief, he said, of the border police.

We rode for what seemed an extraordinarily long time — one was constantly to be astonished by the size of Berlin — standing up and jammed immobile among the usual blue hordes. "I hope," I said, as we went on and on, "that I'm still in the Sector, not the *Zone!*" and when he laughed, one suddenly realized that whatever the reason (Hank was a part of it, one later understood) one felt no uneasiness: in this anomalous arrangement one trusted Ernst. There are times when either this is so or it isn't; one trusts or doesn't trust, at a level above reason; and once it's decided there's no point obviously in speculating about mishaps or holding back.

Eventually we were out again, in another quarter.

This was Berlin-Lichtenburg, with Stalin Allee — apparently one of the Festival specialties — gala with great flags streaming from masts, and all the Uncles on hand again, the giant faces in full force, and quantities of people milling about. We walked some distance, striking off after a while across a wide space now cleared of its rubble; and when I asked where we were headed, for one began to wonder, Ernst said that it was the *Zentralhaus der Jungen Pioniere:* the Young Pioneer House — which was, it seemed, the second of the only two in existence; the other being the original, the model, in Moscow. "We hope all our cities will one day have them. It took much money, much work, to build; but it is built well, for peace not war."

The House, one found, was an impressive sort of place, handsomely erected as if here to stay, and looking, true enough, as if the cost hadn't been counted by those responsible for it. (Klaus was to say, "They have never underestimated the force of the cultural. It is one of the paradoxes! — that they, who enslave, trust *ideas* more than the Americans have seemed to do in Europe. We see the perversion of their arts and artists; but they will never ignore them! we can be sure of that!") It was also, we found, closed; locked up. But Ernst, with a bang or two on the great glass doors — sounding somehow practiced as well as peremptory — summoned a caretaker who at once admitted us and then, as instructed, went off to find someone at an authoritative level.

It was a young woman who appeared, several minutes later. In the inevitable blue shirt, she was muscular, unsmiling; and it was obvious, from the outset, that she couldn't have been less pleased by the sight of me. That I was squired by the police didn't seem to help matters — merely deepening, presumably, the possibilities for treachery; and the fact that Ernst's manner was again exhibiting that touch of proprietorship, even of protection, wasn't calculated, as any woman anywhere knows, to endear one to another woman already put off. She said "Freundschaft!" as if delivering a body blow. And when we shook hands I almost exclaimed Ouch! — not sure (one never was) if the grip was routine or deliberately hardened to expose one's flimsiness! Ernst's request that I be shown throughout the building was just short of a command; only just; and when I said, a bit anxiously, "If you're sure it isn't a bother — " that sounded wrong too; the words trailed off, effete and inept, or serpentinely, perhaps, to a hostile ear. Even the patchwork cotton skirt seemed suddenly unfortunate: a "decadent West" get-up, devised by a neurotic!

We climbed a fine stairway to the first floor.

And now for an hour or so one was literally shown everything: room after immaculate and superbly equipped room, spacious, gleaming, as orderly as the departments in a first-rate museum, and deadly still, with that aggressive emptiness of a building created to house many people with none of them on hand — for we were, apparently, the only ones here, the flint-like young woman, Ernst, myself: a strange trio in a silent place. Our footsteps rang out on the polished floors. The information delivered had a cold thrust to it, as if it were being spoken across a distance or down a tube. Along wide corridors, into room after room: rooms where children made model ships, where they studied plant life, where they painted pictures; a charming room, long-windowed and oval, where little girls were taught ballet dancing, and another, with many small chairs and music stands, for their own orchestra. Rooms outfitted for wood-carving, for clay-modeling, for carpentry; a chemical laboratory; a map room; a library; and a perfect little theatre, a child's dream, replete with footlights and a red velvet curtain.

Everything that one could offhand think of was here; the equipment was superb; the order impeccable.

"You see," Ernst said, "this is what we believe our children should have. And all children everywhere. They make fine things; they learn and work in a good way." And he said, "This you can tell when you return. How our children here have no guns to play with!"

We were standing in a room where radios were assembled. Bigger boys, and even little ones, worked here together; and a radio that had just that day been completed — by three twelve-year-olds, we were told — had been placed "on exhibition," on a central table. When President Pieck came here, as he was to do next week, the little boys were to be allowed to show it to him.

"They must have worked very hard," Ernst said. "That's a big job, for boys so young!"

It seemed to me a quite remarkable job. "Is it theirs?" I asked. "Can they keep what they make?"

The young woman said, "It will be sent to our comrades in Korea."

Along silent corridors, into empty rooms. It was for children, but none of the children were here. Only this custodian,
this guardian of the place: this unrevealed, flint-like girl at
one's side. And gradually it was she who filled the thought;
not the things she was telling one or what was being shown,
but she herself, with her set face. Where had she come from,
through what sort of years? What confusions or bitterness or
blindness or loss? Had she ever heard any other sort of word?
or been touched-through to, by another sign? At that inmost
point, that center which for each of us is the secret place, the
never quite obliterated or altogether told, what did she feel?
what did she seek?

For it was as if, suddenly, she were the child. All alone in
this big house.

I don't know why; why I thought of the words — the passage from Rilke's Cornet Christophe who carried the banner
in a long-ago war.

> He of Langenau writes a letter, deep in thought. Slowly
> he traces the great earnest upright letters:
>   "My kind Mother:
>   be proud: I am the bearer of the standard
>   do not worry: I am the bearer of the standard
>   love me: I am the bearer of the standard — "
> Then he puts away the letter in his coat of mail, in the most
> secret place beside the rose-petal. And he thinks: soon it
> will be fragrant. And he thinks: perhaps someone will find
> it . . . And he thinks . . . : for the foe is at hand.

Why was it strangely as if she were the child? In the coat
of mail. Love me: I am the bearer of the standard. But it
wasn't the shining one; the standard was false; and there was
no one to love her. There was no love here. Suddenly that
was what one knew. In this fine building, there was no love.

When at the entrance again, saying goodbye, for one moment we looked clear at each other — when for one moment she almost smiled — there was something in me that could have wept.

It was late now, still warm and with a lingering of gold in the air, but evening, one realized, well advanced. And suddenly I felt ferociously hungry.

Standing there, on the street, I said, "Ernst, would you come and have supper with my friends — the friends I'm staying with?"

For the first time something happened between us. His look changed; it was piercing, vigilant.

"Why do you ask that?"

"Because I'm starving! Aren't you?"

And because I wished he might meet them — Klaus and Gerhardt and Regina and Tante, my friends who were his countrymen, his fellow Germans.

"I'd like you, all of you, to meet one another."

After a moment he said, "You don't understand."

"Isn't it good for people to meet?"

"You don't understand," he said again. And it was then that I learned that he hadn't been across into West Berlin for almost three years.

"You mean, you're not *permitted to go?*"

He said, as if obliged to explain to a child, "I have much information that would be of value to their police." And all at once his voice might have come from someone else: clenched, harsh. "A friend of mine — " he said. I thought, looking up, it was to be withheld; but he said, "Eight months ago, a friend of mine — he, too, had information they want. That was the end; he has not returned." And his face, one saw, matched his voice. The face of one confronting an unscrupulous foe.

The impact of something was so sharp against the mind that one almost spoke, almost let the words out. *"He is afraid!"* There it was! What he had said he himself believed; he meant it; it was real to him, deadly real. His friend had gone (for whatever the reason: Volkspolizei too were taking refuge across the border). And one heard another voice, equally grim — Klaus telling about a lawyer with whom in some way he had been associated, one inferred, in his secret work: "Six weeks or so ago, near the Brandenburg Gate" — he had been seized and thrust into an East Berlin car. Someone had heard him call out his name. Nothing more. "That's the last we know."

"That's the last we know." "He has not returned." Almost the same words spoken on each side. There — to be credited, in how grave a way. Here — sharpening one's knowledge of a diabolism at work. But the same words; the same fear.

And one found oneself suddenly, and with a kind of gratitude, saying, "Thank you, Ernst, for trusting me!" For one hadn't until now thought of that: that at a certain level it went both ways — with the giving of trust, in this world of his, no small gift.

After that we had dinner, at a HO restaurant, sitting there and talking for a long time. And face to face with him across a bare-board table, one was conscious, in a way one hadn't been before, of this detachment of his; the caliber of it; the force. From the first, of course, it had marked his attitude — in a curious mixture of the casual and the punctilious; and one began to feel now, as a meal was shared, that it had to do with some basic evaluation of the "personal." (In a way and to a degree involving onself; since here one was.) If it, the detachment, struck one as monklike, it was only in terms of discipline, not denial; since obviously, as a type, he was akin to the athlete rigorously in trim rather than to any abstemious ascetic. It was something familiar, and yet not quite familiar. As a woman, one knew the sort of man — with a particular gift or drive or concern — for whom life was necessarily departmentalized, so that he existed, while at work, wholly within the dimensions of that work, and, when he wasn't, more or less wholly in whatever was the essential complement to it. It was as if he alternated between adjacent rooms. But with Ernst, one felt, the arrangement was different. There was the impression that whatever his "personal" life consisted of, it wouldn't supplement, at the same level, his official one. It would remain subsidiary to it, and doubtless expendable; not a *now* this and *now* that back-and-forthness, but *first* of all this and *then* that. It was as if he lived towerlike, up and down, with the top his dedication to a purpose and a task and somewhere almost ignominiously below, the things for "himself."

We sat there talking together, over our empty plates. Not inwardly, and progressively, as one had with Käthe; for here there was no shared frame of reference, and everything spoken of had so fixed an end — his own assertion of the "facts" of the case — that every few minutes one had to start again, with a different question, or from another angle. Until the Russian soldiers happened to be mentioned, the ordinary ones, here in the Sector.

"What are they like, Ernst? Do they and the Germans get together at all?"

Only, he said, when they were out on patrol duty, two by two; otherwise, no. He spoke on a sudden note of reserve; and I asked again, "But what are they like?"

After a moment he said, "In all armies there are men who are not good."

"Yes, I suppose so. In all everything! But aren't they *lonely?* Whenever I see them that's what I think — how *lonely* they look!"

"To be in another people's country," he said, "that is not good, for any man."

"What about me!"

He gestured it aside.

"Well, what about Hank then? He must have been here."

"That, too, was different," he said. And he added, "We were soldiers then, all together."

The remark seemed casually, inadvertently made; and I almost missed it. Soldiers? I said. "But as soldiers weren't you rather busy killing one another!"

"No — afterwards. For that small time." And he said, still without change of tone, "We were all together here — Americans, British, Russian, French; we were soldiers who knew what war is. We could meet," he said, "here in Berlin."

"And that was good?"

"Yes, that was the good time," he said.

It was as if, one realized, something delicately had happened.

And even when he stated, "Now it is different," the moment held: the sense of an *opening*, somewhere in the air; of a sudden *outside*. And one found oneself saying, for the first time in such a way, "Oh, Ernst — but not the people! surely it's not the *people* who're any different — "

Yes, he asserted; the people too. "The Americans here now — they don't know what it's like. They're ignorant. They behave badly, arrogantly, towards us." And he said, as if it were something believed, "They hate us now."

The Americans he hadn't encountered for three years! The unknown men, faceless, voiceless.

One denied the words, since it was a duty to perform, although, by this time, realizing that denials, however mettlesome, appeared to be about as effective as a barrage of hiccoughs. He simply said, straight on, as if one hadn't spoken, "It is different now — you can see for yourself."

The recurrent phrase, one had gradually grown aware; the point that for him was apparently central, as if the fact that one could "see" all this for oneself must operate, automatically, to his advantage. For "Look!" — wasn't that what he had been saying from the first? Look at our magnificent stadium demonstration; look at what our children are being provided with; look (as the truckloads of police went singing past) at those who are called by the West our Army! That one had come here deliberately, *willing* to look, presumably constituted the necessary credentials. That one must, behind the formality of dissent, be unable to gainsay the evidence of one's own eyes, appeared, on his part, to be a solid assumption. "You can see for yourself." There it was. With the advantage his — since he, not I, was the one in a position to exhibit "proof": not talking about something but literally showing it. And one was struck now by the fact that in spite of this rigor of attitude he wasn't in the least concerned with abstractions; on the contrary, wasn't he to an exceptional degree dependent upon the outward, the graspable thing? With Käthe one had moved among concepts and ideas; but hadn't there, with Ernst, right from the start, been this constant and emphatic preoccupation with externals? He hadn't, at the outset, said, "Let us talk"; he had said, "I will show you our Berlin" — because the scene itself was the certainty he moved in; his world, though inexorably shaped by a doctrine, wasn't for him a doctrinaire proposition; it was immediate, concrete; a tangible world; it was even, one gradually began to grasp — and contradicting though this did the impression of detachment — it was even, in a sense, curiously personal. For look at oneself, sitting here like this. One could say (as one kept on saying and saying), "That's not true," or even, "It's a perfectly damnable lie," and not only did the words quite fail to affect him, they also — ironically — so far as one could judge, equally failed to invalidate oneself! As if it were an actual presence that counted. So that the fact that here one was, literally here on this other side, and willing at least to examine his "evidence," successfully outregistered the repudiating of that evidence! One was a *deed* to him, it would seem; not a *declaration*. And one found oneself thinking: in this way he is reached — not by an idea, but by the embodiment of it; an idea in operation. By the act itself. Wasn't that what he was susceptible to? And for three years now everything he had heard and seen and known, and touched with his hands and performed himself, had been *here*, sealed off, uncompared with and unconditioned by anything else: rigid within the framework of a single interpretation.

One said, "No, Ernst, it isn't true," but speaking the words quickly, almost to one side; for the thing he had said — how strange a thing! Delicately, not done with, it seemed to hang there in the air. "That small time — " How very strange! His city in ruins, the alien armies encamped; and he said, looking back, "That was the good time." He said, "Then we were all together."

And it was now that we began to speak of Hank.

"He was here, then, in Berlin — at the end of the war?"

"Yes, very soon; he was one of the first." And he added, as

if wishing one to appreciate the fact, "He had much hard fighting, it was very bad for him before he came."

An American, after much hard fighting, had arrived. And because he had done so, another soldier, a German, the enemy he had fought, had learned to speak English with a Midwest accent.

"Why, Ernst? How did it happen?"

He said, without sentiment, a statement of fact, "He was my friend."

The sequence might naturally have been friendship, then language.

"And was he here a long time?"

"Eleven months, a little more."

And now where was he? "In Nebraska?" one asked — and might, from the effect of it, have uttered an abracadabra sort of word; for instantly, sharply, Ernst was demanding, "You know Nebraska? You have been there, yes?"

I hadn't, as a matter of fact; and explained that it was a long way away from where I lived.

"Yes, I know." His manner suddenly had become authoritative. "It is a very big state, in the middle, with much farm-land."

"And very cold, I believe."

"In the winter, yes. But in the summer very hot." And precisely, as if it were a line being read, he said, "At noon you can fry an egg on the henhouse roof!"

Hank I at once envisioned as a farmer; but he wasn't, apparently, although his father was one, and he himself, until the war, had lived always on a farm — "with grain growing on it, big as a sea." Now, it appeared, he was working in a filling station. "With two other fellows. It's theirs, they own it.

On an Autobahn," Ernst said, "with much traffic going past. Many hundreds of cars in a single day!"

I suppose it was the suddenness, the unexpectedness of the turn. Perhaps the impact of an image, or a word even — "filling station," "henhouse" — for at what slight touch there can flash into the head half a lifetime, or a country: all lucid, particularized; happening between moments. One saw, coming forward, an American garage man — beside a road running clean to where sky touched earth across interminable prairie lands all glittering and moving like a green-gold sea with the plumed wheat, the tasseled corn; and on a road between hills bearing juniper and sumac, dogwood, redbud, or gone blue-berry-blue in August heat with the village green ringed by the clapboard houses and the gilt cock spinning on the meeting-house spire, with walls of stone along a rocky pasture and stones, in the amber shallows of river, palely glinting or frozen away with the shadow of an elm drawn stiff and amethystine on the blank snow; a road beside an islanded and piney coast, and by a golden shore with mountains carrying lupine high like a cloud; and a road across deserts under immensities of sky, with earth the parched crust of a planet among planets, and starkly exposed, in a blaze of space, a universe, a stupendous outwhirl of stars; roads marked by magnolia, redwood, maple; by cotton field and lemon grove and cranberry bog; with the bluejay wheeling, and the mockingbird and the thrush; and the grip of zero and the haze of heat, with hurricane, blizzard, and burst of cloud, and the sun, a bright warrior, storming across the land. . . .

One saw an American garage man step forward.

The blue shirt that didn't mean anything at all, sweaty, grimy, with rolled-up sleeves; the easy grin; the authoritative

service. One heard him saying, "Hi!" saying, "So long!"
Casual, expert, friendly, decent.

America! one almost said out loud.

Sitting here like this in East Berlin, with Ernst who was
chief of the border police.

There was nothing much added to the few things learned.
Nothing remarkable about Hank was to emerge, no revelatory
opinions, no acts of distinction; really nothing at all when one
came right down to it. Ernst said, as if it were sum enough,
"He was a good fellow." A farm boy from Nebraska (lanky?
towheaded? — one never knew) hurtled from his plains into
this dense and complex and undismissable Europe, hard into
the outrageous fact of war. He could scarcely have sounded
more ordinary, more nondescript; unless there was something
about a young American teaching a young German to speak
his language that wasn't altogether without singularity.

I asked again, "But how did it happen, Ernst? How did
you meet?"

"He was lost, in his jeep. I took him back."

"And then you became friends?"

"Then we became friends."

Two soldiers who only a few weeks before had been
pledged, each of them, to destroy the other. Well, there it
was. And after all, why not? Life was full of the most
astounding simplicities; it was all made up of marvel and
miracle, happening hourly, casual as light. And suddenly
Hank, in his very ordinariness, seemed something tremendous.
He had crossed an ocean, and fought in a war; he had made a
friend — nothing more than that; and yet, because of it, because of his coming and being what he was, one sat here now,
several years afterwards. For wasn't that the reason this had

come to pass? Or an essential part of the reason at any rate. Wasn't it because there had been a Hank that Ernst, yesterday, had broken through the crowd, to another American, stranded too, and asked in his English, "Can I help?"

And one thought: how intermeshed we all are! wherever we stand, and whoever we may be; and how nobody knows the wholeness of the pattern made, but perceives as yet, through a glass darkly, only the inkling: only the fragmentary and the fugitive thing. And aloud one said, "Isn't it strange! Here we sit, talking about Hank, and he, in Nebraska — perhaps, who knows, he's talking about you, saying, 'In Berlin I had a friend — ' " And it was then that Ernst spoke of the offer that had come.

"He wanted me to go out there."

I didn't grasp it at once.

"To Nebraska," he said. "He wanted me to work with them at the filling station."

Two years ago, it seemed, the letter had come.

"Oh, Ernst! — he *did!* — "

He said at once, and incisively, "I am needed, here in Germany. There is work to be done."

Which was true; which one believed oneself in a different way; for surely the solution couldn't properly lie in a Europe drained of all the hardy ones and the spirited.

"But for a little while, Ernst! Just to see what it's like!"

And suddenly it seemed something of inexpressible importance.

"To meet people! really meet them, and find out about everything — " And his own words all at once could be driven back at him, hard. "To see for yourself!" And one asked directly, "Are you afraid of that, Ernst! — of doing what I'm doing over here?"

He didn't answer for some moments; and when he said, briefly, "I would not be allowed to," the statement seemed to close on him, like a physical grip. Here he existed, held in a vise. And one almost exclaimed, wanting to strike out against everything in sight, "But it can't — not *forever* — go on like this! Oh, Ernst! it must be *you* — it must be *your* decision — "

"I would not be allowed into your country," he said.

There had been, with Liesl, that spasm of hopelessness: not knowing how to break through to her through the blur of of lies. Now it was different. Now for the first time, hearing him say that, there was something one hadn't until this point felt. A kind of despair; a kind of rage. One thought of Ernst working at the filling station by the road; one saw, in a great cavalcade, Americans going past — "Hi!" they were saying to him, from the trucks and the Cadillacs and the converted jeeps, with twangs and drawls and in a score of accents: the Americans who had come, whoever they were, every man jack of them, without exception — at some point in their ancestry or in their own experience — from somewhere else, from the rest of the world: from a manor house on a knoll and a jungle hut, from slum and rice paddy and olive grove and potato patch; from tundra and mountain and seacoast and steppes, and intimate parish and university tower. Americans — endlessly streaming past; with Ernst in a blue shirt polishing their windshields; Ernst eating hamburgers and gulping cokes, and sitting in the evening on people's porches, with the creak of a rocking chair, and a lawnmower sending up a green spray of grass, and the children in the late light, out in the street, playing hopscotch, or pitching balls, or skipping into ropes with little rhymes that all ended in a pounce with "*out!*" Ernst having supper in neighbors' houses, with

succotash and squash and hominy grits (or ravioli and chop
suey and tamales and Wurst), with newspapers strewn on the
living-room davenport and the radio, in a blare, gabbling,
clarifying, vulgarizing, challenging, with a ballgame outballoon-
ing the atom bomb and a deodorant discussed as pressingly
as God. Ernst being asked by the local Something-or-Other
to give a speech — "I Chose Nebraska," or "My Youth Behind the Curtain" — or standing on the farm that was "big
as a sea," looking off and off and off into space. One saw him
in Washington, in a springtime dusk, on the steps below the
great grave Lincoln in his chair. And in the gilt-and-scarlet of
a New England autumn, at Concord, leaning against the
little bridge with the greeny-bronze Minute Man just at hand
— that other young man who'd had a hard thing to do, and
had done it well, and was marked here now by nothing grandiose, nothing martial or even very dramatic: only a small
bridge across a reedy river, and the bronze farmer-soldier with
musket and plow, and a little way away, beyond a quiet field,
the gray Old Manse with the elms under which one would sit
with Ernst (as we had one April with Hildegard and her
brothers) reading Thoreau aloud, reading the Emerson who
with his clear eye and fine beak had walked this town and
whose words Hans had turned to in his notebook at
Berchtesgaden —

*"The power which is at once spring and regulator in all
efforts of reform, is the conviction that there is an infinite
worthiness in man which will appear at the call of worth, and
that all particular reforms are the removing of some impediment . . . not by the men or the material the statesman uses,
but by men transfigured and raised above themselves by the
power of principles."*

And one saw oneself now, in a hare-brained sort of way —

popping up in Washington, on Capitol Hill, and saying to certain persons: "Please, I should like three visas for three friends. Their names are Liesl, Käthe, and Ernst. One of them holds a responsible position in the Volkspolizei, which is the East German People's Police; and another was some kind of minor official in the Soviet World Youth Festival for Peace; and the third is a girl who had a grisly sort of experience, and is terrified inside of there being another war; terrified, that is, that America will start one. I should like them to come here and stay with me for a while — although one of them would be off in Nebraska for a time."

"Three *friends* of yours, do we understand you to say?"

"Well, perhaps not friends. But we touched through somehow — it's a little difficult to explain."

"Three Germans who are *Communists?*"

"Yes, that's right. That's why I'm so anxious to have them come."

One could hear the cavalrylike clatter in the corridors: a rush of commitees, hair on end.

"Are you actually proposing that we let into *the United States of America* — "

And now one saw the United States of America: one hundred and sixty million strong, and ranged against it, Liesl, Käthe, Ernst, in a row.

" — that you would deliberatcly bring here our *avowed enemies!* You would expose your own country — "

"Please, no; the other way around. I'd expose three people, who don't know it, to my country."

" — at a time like this, when the duty of every loyal citizen in the land is to fearlessly unearth — "

But there's nothing to unearth about Käthe and Ernst! There they are — they couldn't be plainer. One might as well fearlessly unearth Mr. Vishinsky!"

"And yet, admitting this, you propose such a thing —
deliberately to flood the United States — "

"Oh, come now, really!"

— "jeopardizing our security, perverting our own youth —"

"You mean *Ernst* would pervert *Hank?* Then what's the
matter with Hank? What on earth's he stuffed with — junket
and jello? And how *could* three people flood three thousand
miles! It's three people, remember? Three particular young
people. Not anybody, and not everybody. Not a Simonov or
an Ehrenburg — or the man in the Berolinahaus who, heaven
knows, only an idiot wouldn't be on guard against. It's Käthe
and Liesl and Ernst, that's all. And if we can't any longer
tell about human beings — if we've really so lost all moral
acuteness, all precision of insight, that we literally can't dis-
criminate between degrees of darkness, between *conditions
of thought* — if this is what's happened to our society and
to ourselves — "

But anger was no use; for how difficult for us all; for the
committees too who must be men, like other men, at times
deeply troubled; and how muddled and ineffectual one's appeal must sound; how futile a thing.

Except that even three — mustn't they be tried for?

"I know they're only three, and not headline stuff; history,
I suppose, won't be changed by any one of them. It's not
much of a haul out of a teeming world. But even *three* less
Communists — or three less people on any wrong track —
isn't that to the good? Isn't it something we might even all
manage to be glad about?"

"But you've just been telling us that they *are* Communists!"

"And so they are. That's what I mean. That's the challenge
they present — the test of ourselves. Because here they

stand, within reach, these three. There are millions upon
millions of others we don't know about, going back and back
into places we can't penetrate; but these are on the rim, at
the soft outer edge; and they're still in the first stages, because it's happened to them late — caught each of them at
some point, and for a different kind of reason, where fear and
idealism and ignorance are all mixed. They're still within ear-
shot; still within touch. They're not yet irretrievable — and
if we can't retrieve *them*, if we can't make sense to those who
are reachable — in Europe or Asia or Timbuctoo — if we're
failing to communicate, where communication's still possible,
the values and verities we believe to be universal — what on
earth makes us think that a world can be won? All the hordes
beyond hordes and hordes of humanity. Where do we start,
that's all I ask? We can expose and denounce at the top of
our lungs — and that must be done; that's part of the job.
But if they're all *still here* — the tragically deluded — if they
still walk the earth with us, unconvinced and unconverted — "

"And you presume to believe you could convert these
three?"

"I presume to believe that the truth converts. I believe
that reforms are the removing of some impediment, and that
there is, in man, a worthiness that will appear at the call of
worth. I believe — "

What? what did one believe? "In salvation" — could that
be said through the halls? And that risks must be taken, high
risks in life, on faith and by grace, or it's a dead thing we live;
and that no one is irredeemably cast off, or doomed; no one
at all.

Now we were outside again, with night fully fallen; a warm
summer night in this other place. We stood together some-

where near Stalin Allee; and in the darkness, faintly and in-
frequently lit, it was as if the explicit impacts of the day,
and everything that had happened in the days before, the
incessant surge upon surge of crowds, and the innumerable
contacts and the many words spoken, were translated now
into a different kind of effect. All was still pulsatingly here
in the dark; but quiescent, quietened; with a closeness that
was less an impression received than a literal sensation: a
closeness so close that it was as if the air breathed were the
breath, just emitted, from other nostrils and any start or even
stir must pull the whole tissue of us at the same moment the
same way. Untold people were here, all around. Visible, some
of them — for they were moving up and down, up and down
in the road, a ghostly restlessness between the dimmed-out
flags; and some distance away, to the sound of music, there
were, one realized, shadowy figures dancing in a rubble-cleared
space (but not many of them, and not vary gala at that; not
as one had often seen Germans dance). There were other
people, nearer, around a Limonade stall, mutedly talking and
indistinguishable from one another, with their faces, as they
lifted them to the tilted bottles, papery discs in the flicker
of light, like the faces, moodless, without age and unsexed,
that ebb in and out at the margin of a dream. All of them,
and everything, had a spectral look. As if one had passed into
a region of shades: a world impalpable and yet in some way
massive; condensations of darkness without form and void
and yet a presence; sentient; a great breathing all around; and
oneself deep within it, deeply inside — For suddenly one
seemed to be, not at the edge, not just across a line, but
drawn without moving far off, far back. One tried to think
of Tante and Stephen and Klaus, sitting on the balcony drinking Nescafé, with Regina playing Mozart in the lighted room;

but they might have been a thousand miles from one now, utterly out of reach and even permanently lost. One was here, in the dark, in strange depths of night. Beyond anybody's hearing or sight or touch. If one shouted, or ran, there would be no help, there'd be nowhere to go since everywhere would be *this*, and even Ernst — who was Ernst? A shadow; a myth. No more to be verified than the ghost-drift of figures, or the phantom dancers in their blank space. And suddenly, urgently, one turned, looking up — grasping at the certainty of sky overhead.

In their appointed places, the stars all stood. Clear, true, exactly fixed.

There as one had known them long ago as a child, getting secretly out of bed to stare from windows, in countries newly come to with the earth still strange; as Socrates had known them from a shapely place, and Columbus on his ship and the boy Shakespeare by a river, and Joan with her angels, and Nicodemus coming to Jesus by night. Above East Berlin all the stars shone clear.

One stood looking up, touching base again. From anywhere at all a man could look up.

And one suddenly said, "Ernst —"needing to speak; needing to include him, that he might be real again. "The same stars," one said, "in Nebraska too." Without turning, one could feel the lift of his head; we were looking up together. *Together*, one thought. And all at once, in that moment, at the point of a shared truth, something seemed to flash plain.

It was the *togetherness* that must be found.

Wasn't that the challenge?

Essentially, and crucially, at this particular hour?

For at each great turn, each move in history, wasn't there a demand that — without excluding other demands — was pre-eminently posed? A particularity of the time? An aspect of the truth? Not created by the era in which it was perceived (since it must, if absolute, timelessly exist) but, at some point of transparency in consciousness, *let through*, as it were, into human visibility: so that each age had its accent, and responsibility; its peculiar and inescapable part to perform in an immense act of recognition. To acknowledge the particular facet and task wasn't to forfeit, or to extract from, the whole. Or, if this did happen, how familiar the result! The usurping dogmas, isolated and atrophied; not flowering into the next expansion of light but immemorially clenched against further unfoldments. This was the hazard, not the fact itself. Since all verities (if verities there were at all) must exist not only in relation to a source — as logically inseparable from it as rays from the sun — but, when accurately enough perceived, must be fitly and indisseverably related to one another. One truth couldn't arise at the expense of another truth. Even if the emphasis, in the long emergence of truths, fell now on this aspect and now on the next, until the thing newly seen was apprehended and bodied forth. In acknowledging one's time one didn't single out a part. But neither could it be evaded — the particularized demand; it could no more be mentally stopped short of by us, if we were to succeed, or even survive, than could the jet-plane pilot be keyed to Kitty Hawk. For wasn't that what we were confronted with at this momentous hour: the challenge not only to occupy our era, not even just to conduct ourselves well within it, but *to appraise with precision the assignment that was ours —*

And all the words seemed suddenly to sound in one's head. The words that had been pounding like a pulse through these airs. "Fellowship," "unity," "co-operation," "of the world" — "Now we have learned that the people is a great brother-

hood" — "all of us together" — "everywhere" and "all." And
"Freundschaft! Freundschaft! Freundschaft siegt!" — with
the tremendous throng singing its anthem in the sun, the
lifted arms linked in a circle without a break and tears on the
young faces and the voices, mingled, all outflying, upwinging,
in a great singleness of sound, as the birds with that beautiful
beat from the ground had flown into the illimitable spaces
of the sky.

The words that meant everybody, not one alone.

The appropriated words — being raised, among the restless and the ignorant and the confused, like the shining banner of Cornet Christophe. Words ringing across the earth,
rallying, *being heard.* For wasn't that the fact? The stark
evidence to be faced? However falsely spoken, the words were
being heard. Because striking to some need at the very heart
of men; some rightness of instinct, however barbarously mis-
used. And did we see this clearly and fearlessly enough?
Were we accurately enough reading the impulses involved?
For suddenly it was as if we were in some way lagging, and
not meeting with exactness a specific claim. The words we
spoke back were stupendous words. They were among the
most glorious shaped by men. Freedom — liberty — independence — the individual. On what fields they had been forged!
in what blazing caverns of the mind, the heart, and at outposts of vision unfailingly besieged. They were among the
most noble words in the world. But they weren't the full
statement. They were only half.

One stood here now, in this shadowy place. A few minutes
before one had felt the falsity; had been lost, drowned out
in an almost suffocating sense of presence and pressure, feeling something of what the negation of identity must be like.
The counterfeit fellowship. The dark fusion that was allied

to chaos and old night. One had stood here, experiencing it, and it was an evil thing. But the answer to that — the logical refutation of *man as mass* — was it only the concept of *individual man?* Even one's own first instinct here had been (when clear again) to speak to Ernst: to establish in the face of that blind absorption not only oneself, one's own identity, but a reality of relationship. That too. And wasn't that the indispensable other half? And what was wanted, needed, by everyone, everywhere? To "liberate" humanity into isolated bits — to say, "There you are, a free man on your own!" — what did it mean at this turn of an hour? Freedom, liberty, independence — yes; but for what? What purpose? Freedom to be an ego or an atom on the loose? To rattle around pea-like in a giant universe? Against the challenge of the mass, of man falsely related, even against the fact of literal enslavement, was freedom of itself the sufficient answer? A man ostensibly in every way "free" could put a bullet through his brains, or lose his nerve, or beat his wife; he could lead a life that was meagre, crippled, distraught, shapeless or heartless or consumed with caution, or quietly desperate as perhaps many lives were. Freedom of itself, what did it mean? And even to keep saying "the individual" as we did, to keep saying it exclusively — was that the way?

And one thought: we must answer with the exact counter-fact. Against *collective* man there was *man universal.* Against the *wrong* relationship there was the relationship that was *right.* Nobody wanted to be an orphan or a bastard. A world wasn't looking for a lonely apartness. (Even the conspirators needed one another, and what criminal remained long without an accomplice?) And if we failed to perceive this, or depended wrongly upon our words — how tremendous the field for the voices that said, not "I" but "us," not "mine" but "ours," that said, out of darkness, "Brothers, come — "

And one thought now: the heart seeks the right thing, but in what ignorance it moves — feeling, as if they were here in the night, the immense dim multitudes on the face of the earth, stirring, seething, coming to themselves: beginning to ask, in confusion and violence, the questions that not a power in the world could stop. "Brothers, come — " The words were going out. *But it's we*, one thought, *it's we who should be saying them!* A thousand times more ringingly than we'd yet begun to. For how utterly without hope this counterfeit thing: trying, at the level of billions of different beings, billions of little wills and minds and metabolisms, trying from the faulty stuff of humanity, to create what could only be inwardly awakened to: individually perceived and in fellowship expressed — that man who because he is acknowledged as a son is therefore brother unto all other men.

And one thought of all the words that there were to speak, and of how old they were, and familiar, and unlistened to — or was that the truth? did one really believe that? Wasn't the listening enormously going on, perhaps as never before in the world? The waiting, the readiness, the hands held out. And one thought of what a Paul might say again, not on Mars' hill but here, like this, here in the night on Stalin Allee. Ye men of Athens — ye men of Berlin —

I perceive that in all things ye are too superstitious. For as I passed by and beheld your devotions, I found an altar with this inscription. TO THE UNKNOWN GOD. Whom therefore ye ignorantly worship, him declare I unto you. God that made the world and all things therein . . . hath made of one blood

all nations of men for to dwell on all the face of the earth . . .
that they should seek the Lord, if haply they might feel after
him, and find him, though he be not far from every one of
us; for in him we live and move and have our being as certain
also of your own poets have said, For we are also his off-
spring. . . .

For as the body is one, and hath many members, and all
the members of that one body, being many, are one body so
also is Christ. For by one Spirit are we all baptized into one
body, whether we be Jews or Gentiles, whether we be bond
or free. . . . For the body is not one member, but many. If
the foot shall say, Because I am not the hand, I am not of the
body; is it therefore not of the body? And if the ear shall say,
Because I am not the eye, I am not of the body; is it therefore not of the body? If the whole body were an eye, where
were the hearing? If the whole were hearing, where were the
smelling? But now God hath set the members every one of
them in the body, as it hath pleased him. . . . And the eye
cannot say unto the hand, I have no need of thee: nor again
the head to the feet, I have no need of you . . . but God hath
tempered the body together . . . that there should be no
schism in the body but that the members should have the
same care one for another.

Now therefore you are no more strangers and foreigners, but
fellow-citizens with the saints, and of the household of God.
And are built upon the foundation of the apostles and the
prophets, Jesus Christ himself being the chief corner stone;
in whom all the building fitly framed together groweth unto
an holy temple in the Lord. In whom ye also are builded
together —

Builded together. But not from a blueprint devised by
ourselves. Wasn't that the radical and everlasting difference?

By divine decree; under unalterable law; and unto a unity awakened to — not with a great song (although the song might come afterwards, as affirmation) — but at an inmost center of identity, of being; at that point in consciousness where each of us must start, and, starting, must find with the truth about himself that which is indivisibly true about all. The shared household; the city of God.

And one thought, walking here in a darkling place, underneath the symbol-steadfastness of the stars, of the words that were spoken before Paul's words, the gentle ones, the tender, going luminously through a world. "And other sheep I have which are not of this fold: them also I must bring, and they shall hear my voice; and there shall be one fold, and one shepherd." One shepherd and one fold. Because love exists. Because of that primary and incandescent fact, that force inextinguishably at the heart of life: that love which seeks out, as well as waiting to be found, saying, "Children, come — " throughout time and throughout space. And one thought, too, of what we are told, "and seeing the multitudes, he went up into a mountain — " It was from the mount that the irradiating call was given; from the mount that they were addressed, all the people, all the pilgrims. And could there be any other way under the sun? Could the brotherhood make sense unless derived from a Father? Unless man were blessedly related to a source, from where could it come — the glad relationship of men?

One walked through a dark and difficult place; but thinking, without hindrance, what can be thought anywhere.

VIII

It was early in the evening, at the end of the last day; for in the morning I was to leave Berlin with my friends — going first to Friedl in her Hessian village, then to Hildegard in Munich, and then back to Berchtesgaden. On the S-Bahn platform there was a packed mass of people; everybody seemed headed in the same direction, and two trains came and went without my being able to get anywhere near them, even with Ernst trying to command a passage. And suddenly, with impatience, he said, "Here, over here — " and crossing the platform, to the opposite side, he got us just in time on to another train.

"But it's going the wrong way!"

"We'll change," he said, "later." (I never did altogether understand the S-Bahn.) And when I leaned against the door, for we were standing as usual, he said, "This way it's best — we'll find you a seat."

Several platforms were passed, equally thronged; we were swinging, it appeared, into a part of the city that I couldn't remember having seen before; and when after a while we got out again it was at a station with relatively few people to cope with. Here Ernst explained to me what I must do. It was simple enough doubtless; but I suppose I was feeling rather tired at this point — the hours behind us had been crowded, without a break; and anyhow I'm not much good with directions — because it all began confusingly to whirl in my head and I must, I suppose, have looked confused; for when the train we were waiting for came to a halt, suddenly, instead of putting me on it by myself, he stepped aboard too.

There were seats, as he'd predicted. Which was just as well — as the journey now seemed to go on and on (with another change? or was it two? or perhaps no change at all: nothing in retrospect very clearly emerges) and I must towards the end have blurred off a bit, for when he said, "We're here, this is the one," and I again looked around, properly aware, the compartment we were in was almost empty.

Ernst himself was sitting opposite in his dark suit. Once before he had appeared in it, out of uniform; and on that occasion, as on this, I hadn't noticed immediately; the impression one received remaining somehow just the same. He was sitting there opposite. And I saw, with some surprise, that since I'd last glanced at him he had put on glasses, dark ones, that hadn't until now been sported and that struck one as rather odd, considering the hour, for both inside and out the air had begun greenly deepening into dusk.

"How mysterious you look, Ernst!"

He had turned from the window, facing inward, towards the aisle.

He said, speaking rapidly, "When we get out, talk English — loudly. And hold my arm."

For a moment I didn't grasp what on earth he meant. Then suddenly it was realized: where we were.

The half-emptied train was slowing down. Outside on a platform one could see other people, nondescript Berliners, in dull-colored clothes, and police in little groups; Western police. Getting up, we stood waiting side by side at the door. Neither of us spoke; there seemed nothing to be said. One could feel him, standing there, immobile and intent; the intentness seemed almost a contraction of the air, and all at once, and bewilderingly, one was shaken with concern —

bewilderingly, because it was for him, for Ernst. *"Let no harm fall —"* Was that what one thought? The door opened in front of us. We stepped outside. And taking his arm, I said loudly, quickly, "How fortunate we've been, haven't we, with — such fine weather, because it does make such a difference —" As we passed three of the police, casually standing there, I could feel his arm, against my hand, go suddenly rigid.

There was another train in, directly opposite us across the platform, ready to leave, and headed back into the East. Swiftly, and just audibly, Ernst said, " — Wiedersehen!" In a matter of moments he had streaked across the space, and past a door that already had begun to close. Inside, he swung around. There was just time to see him. His arm lifted, in a gesture of farewell.

I held up my own arm. The train drew out.

"Auf Wiedersehen! Auf Wiedersehen!" one hadn't called. "Danke schön, Ernst —" Danke schön, mein Freund.

The tracks were bare again. People left, and others came; the police paced casually, chatting with one another. One went on standing there, in a stillnes of one's own. It had happened so abruptly, and for only moments; that was all. One had scarcely before it was over realized what it meant. But he had brought one back. He had come this way.

Ernst, in friendship, had crossed the line.

JOURNEY GOING ON

And God hath spread the earth as a carpet for you,
that ye may walk therein through spacious paths.

KORAN *IXXI*

The angels keep their ancient places, —
Turn but a stone and start a wing!
'Tis ye, 'tis your estranged faces,
That miss the many-splendoured thing.

FRANCIS THOMPSON

Thus this universe of ours is a wonder of power and wisdom,
everything by a noiseless path coming to pass according to
a law that none may elude — which the base man never con-
ceives though it is leading him, all unknowingly, to that place
in the All whither he must be borne; which the just man knows
and, knowing, sets forth, understanding before he departs
where he shall be housed in the end.

PLOTINUS

In this country the sun shineth night and day;
wherefore this was beyond the Valley of the
Shadow of Death, and also out of the reach of
Giant Despair; neither could they from this
place so much as see Doubting Castle. Here
they were within sight of the City they were
going to: also here met them some of the inhabitants therof. For in this land the shining ones commonly walked, because it was upon
the borders of Heaven.

JOHN BUNYAN

The Peace of the celestial city is the perfectly ordered and
harmonious enjoyment of God and one another in God.

ST. AUGUSTINE

JOURNEY GOING ON

WE CAME DOWN from the mountains on the great swinging road.

Ahead of us, to be reached that evening, was Trieste; and already Kip must have started from Venice for our converging point on the Piazza del Unita with its café tables and chairs, spidery elegant in the sun, and the pigeons in clouds and the Adriatic peacock blue. Beyond there was Yugoslavia, a whole country, awaiting us. Zagreb, Dubrovnik — names shaped in a different way; and people who would speak differently and act with a difference, and be called not Liesl and Käthe and Ernst, but Drago, Nadya, Miloje, Koca; with minarets against the sky, and left bleached and silent among the rosemary and thyme the broken columns, the stone steps, of Greece and Rome; and the dazzle of white dust; and the figs in the little trees — hanging fatly, green and purple, as for a thousand years, with the grapes still borne down a sunlit slope like an antique poem on the slanted back of a singing girl. A whole new country — and everything it meant. All there; all mattering; all waiting to be received, and, as received, becoming part of one's very self.

We drove down and down through a stark stone world. The sun struck out, and then a violence of rain; and then there was fog again, flying blindly through the air and again dissolving or like a ghost flying on. Down and down from the mountains we had touched. And gradually the high steep meadows reappeared: the miracle of green after glacier and rock, and in flood beyond flood the Alpine flowers, so delicate and precise, so perfectly wrought that they matched as marvel, the utmost heights. Rain and sun and the cold flying mists; and the road looping back on itself and swinging down; until at some point, later, in the middle of the day, it all fully cleared, all the sky and air, and we found ourselves coming, at a sudden turn, into a valley beyond which other mountains stood, fabulous and glittering, in romantic shapes — "The Dolomites?" I asked; but the Dolomites were farther off — and holding somewhere the pass into Italy that we were headed for.

The valley lay below us, all wide and fair. All golden it was; so Psalmlike a scene, so bright, so fresh, so candidly and serenely spread in the sun, that one might have been looking into a childhood landscape, innocently inherited, without strain or strife, with not a mark on it anywhere, not a shadow in sight, as if in all the length of it there was nothing even known of hurt or of harm or grief or fear: as if all who walked here were kind and good, and dwelled together in gentleness and security and joy. We stopped on the road, and sat quietly, looking down. And now one could hear in the immense stillness of the air the faint and crystalline sound of bells. A few villages could be seen, and the spires of churches. It was Sunday, we remembered; and the bells were calling out.

They sang back and forth, very faint and pure, and above them, in the sky, there was the singing of birds. No one was to be seen; no one at all. The valley could be peopled in whatever way one chose. The gilded earth, and the bells, and the flowers that grew, and the simplicity of it and the innocence; here it widely lay. And the inhabitants could be the inhabitants one had known as a child. All walked in uprightness, in garments of praise. All shone; all were trusted; every hand was clasped . . . in the golden streets the children were all singing like the birds. . . .

We sat there quietly. And one thought again how the moments are forever here to be found, by each of us as we journey, and no matter how we come; no matter where we start from or at what point in time, or how defaced we may appear by the names we bear. For at the moments, at the breakthrough, there is no lesser thing; only this; only now; without process or past, and so immune to the multitudes behind one or ahead. All may be seen as freshly as if never before seen. For each, after all, is his own first time. Each, at some inmost point in himself, must stand, must exist, at a common start. Not lost in a sequence; but singly sprung. The primal pilgrim — whether early or late: with the discoveries undiminished by the discoverers who have passed; the verities still dawnlike; the very leaf and bird as green, as singing, anywhere found, as the bird and leaf first loosed into light.

After a while we started again; on our way.